T0328444

Cambridge Elements ☰

Elements in Environmental Humanities
edited by
Louise Westling
University of Oregon
Serenella Iovino
University of North Carolina at Chapel Hill
Timo Maran
University of Tartu

ECOSEMIOTICS

The Study of Signs in Changing Ecologies

Timo Maran
University of Tartu

CAMBRIDGE
UNIVERSITY PRESS

CAMBRIDGE
UNIVERSITY PRESS

University Printing House, Cambridge CB2 8BS, United Kingdom

One Liberty Plaza, 20th Floor, New York, NY 10006, USA

477 Williamstown Road, Port Melbourne, VIC 3207, Australia

314–321, 3rd Floor, Plot 3, Splendor Forum, Jasola District Centre,
New Delhi – 110025, India

79 Anson Road, #06–04/06, Singapore 079906

Cambridge University Press is part of the University of Cambridge.

It furthers the University's mission by disseminating knowledge in the pursuit of
education, learning, and research at the highest international levels of excellence.

www.cambridge.org
Information on this title: www.cambridge.org/9781108931939
DOI: 10.1017/9781108942850

First published 2020

A catalogue record for this publication is available from the British Library.

ISBN 978-1-108-93193-9 Paperback
ISSN 2632-3125 (online)
ISSN 2632-3117 (print)

Ecosemiotics

The Study of Signs in Changing Ecologies

Elements in Environmental Humanities

DOI: 10.1017/9781108942850
First published online: November 2020

Timo Maran
University of Tartu
Author for correspondence: Timo Maran, timo.maran@ut.ee

Abstract: This Element provides an accessible introduction to ecosemiotics and demonstrates its pertinence for the study of today's unstable culture–nature relations. Ecosemiotics can be defined as the study of sign processes responsible for ecological phenomena. The arguments in this Element are developed in three steps that take inspiration from both humanities and biological sciences: 1) Showing the diversity, reach, and effects of sign-mediated relations in the natural environment from the level of a single individual up to the functioning of the ecosystem. 2) Demonstrating numerous ways in which prelinguistic semiotic relations are part of culture and identifying detrimental environmental effects that self-contained and purely symbol-based sign systems, texts, and discourses bring along. 3) Demonstrating how ecosemiotic analysis centered on models and modeling can effectively map relations between texts and the natural environment, or the lack thereof, and how this methodology can be used artistically to initiate environmentally friendly cultural forms and practices.

Keywords: ecosemiotics, ecosystem, culture, semiotic modelling, nature writing

Isbns: 9781108931939 (PB), 9781108942850 (OC)
Issns: 2632–3125 (online), 2632–3117 (print)

Contents

Introduction

What have environmental humanities and global ecological crises to do with semiotics? For most readers with a background in the humanities, the word "semiotics" probably brings to mind Roland Barthes, Michael Foucault, Umberto Eco, Jacques Derrida, and other authors of European semiology and post-structuralism. This tradition, which peaked in the 1970s, treated signs as building blocks of human culture. By highlighting the conventionality of meaning, it provided tools for critical analysis of culture, society, and their power dynamics. This Element, however, will take a different route. Semiotics has much to offer to environmental humanities, but for this some of its philosophical and conceptual underpinnings need to be revised. Most importantly, in this Element signs are treated not as fully conventional and arbitrary means of human culture, but as partly rooted in the natural world and in our corporality. In thinking about nonhuman nature, I rely on the biosemiotic tradition that has been arguing for the existence of semiotic processes on different levels of the biological world ranging from cells to ecosystems, and both inside and between organisms. In particular, I make use of the writings by Jakob von Uexküll, Jesper Hoffmeyer, Almo Farina, and Kalevi Kull. In the ecosemiotic view, semiotic processes are seen as shaped by available conditions, encumbered by their history, yet at the same time as partly autonomous and independent. This allows connecting semiotics with approaches that acknowledge the role of agency, communication, and information in animals and ecosystems.

Ecosemiotics as a branch of semiotics emerged in the mid 1990s to scrutinize semiosic or sign-mediated aspects of ecology (including relations between human culture and ecosystems). It has been defined as "the study of sign processes which relate organisms to their natural environment" (Nöth 2001: 71) or as the semiotic discipline investigating "human relationships to nature which have a semiosic (sign-mediated) basis" (Kull 1998: 351). This means that ecosemiotics is one of the semiotic theories that extends the scope of a central concept of semiotics – the sign (understood as a mediated relation) – from human culture to other species and, particularly, to ecological systems. More recently, ecosemiotics has been specified as "a branch of semiotics that studies sign processes as responsible for ecological phenomena." (Maran and Kull 2014: 41) The concern of ecosemiotics may be considered to lie with the semiotic processes that relate to or address the broader context of living biological processes (Maran 2017a: 5).

The first section of this Element highlights the semiotic nature of ecosystems by scrutinizing semiotic relations between organisms (mostly focusing on animals) and the environment, intra- and interspecies communicative relations, and the role of semiosis in ecosystems. Although such a semiotic take on ecology may remain somewhat technical, it serves as an important foundation for ecosemiotic argumentation. Demonstrating the semiotic nature of ecosystems allows us first to show that there is a vast semiotic realm that surrounds human culture and that we can relate to it through our everyday activities and cultural processes. Secondly, the semiotic approach to ecology allows us to comprehend that what are commonly described as ecological problems often have semiotic causes. They may be, in fact, semiotic problems – as in semiotic pollution (Posner 2000), in which human usage of sound and light interferes with the perception and communication of other species. And thirdly, connecting semiotics and ecology is a way of bringing issues of materiality, resources, and biological corporality into the humanities, which, in my understanding, is a prerequisite for working on solutions to the current ecological crises. That is, the healing and integrating of our episteme can only occur in two simultaneous ways: by arguing for the semiotic character and significance of the environment; and by showing the materiality, liveliness, and resource dependence of human culture.

The second section focuses on the criticism of the striving toward a fully conventional and symbolic human culture that has been a characteristic feature of modernity. Here, I treat culture as a sum of human creative, modeling, and transforming activities and leave the important topic of animal cultures aside. In ecosemiotics, Kalevi Kull (1998) has shown that human culture inevitably changes nature as our actions toward nature are motivated by our sign-based distinctions. A more abstract and self-contained culture results in more contrived actions, which lead to the impoverishment of ecosystems. At the same time, semiotic analysis allows us to demonstrate that the ideal of a self-contained and autonomous culture has never succeeded, and that different levels of cultural systems include presymbolic semiotic entities. In this argumentation I find partners in dialogue among such authors as Alf Hornborg, Kalevi Kull, Michel Serres, Ronald Posner, and Michael Polanyi. The presence of presymbolic icons and indexes, tacit signs, onomatopoeia, and environmental–cultural hybrid signs is not just the reality of culture, but most necessary for retaining sustainable relations between human culture and ecosystems, as well as for the dynamics and rejuvenation of the culture itself. Both Juri Lotman's understanding of communication as cultural creativity and Gregory Bateson's epistemology of the sacred have indicated that normal functioning of culture depends on the dialogue with what lies outside of cultural codes and hierarchies. Therefore, it is indeed necessary to support the practices and processes that foster culture's interaction with sign activities going on in the rest of the ecosystem.

Semiotics also provides us with the means to understand and analyze the capacities of cultural artefacts – literary works, fine art, media texts – to relate with sign processes in the ecosystem. Here, the cultural semiotics of Juri Lotman offers a way to proceed. Lotman's cultural semiotics includes several concepts with ecological potential, e.g. semiosphere, cultural boundary, and semiotics of space, but what is most relevant among these is probably the idea of semiotic modeling. The third section discusses the possibilities of using semiotic modeling as a tool to reconfigure culture–nature relations. The model is understood here as a cultural artefact that, on the one hand, has its own autonomy by having been compiled on the basis of cultural codes and languages. On the other hand, the model has an analogy-based relationship with the object to which it relates – be it the natural environment, human life history, or social groups. The analogy of the model is, however, always construed on a certain ground that is often the basic cultural image or mode of thinking. Now, analyzing the grounds for cultural models provides us with an effective tool for understanding from where the models come, how they work, and what their effects on culture–nature relations are. In this discussion, I use examples from literary works while acknowledging that a similar approach is applicable in film, art, and other cultural domains. Modeling theory also has a prescriptive potential as it enables us to create new bases of comparison that can be used to build new types of models to make sense of the ecosystem. Here, modeling theory can be seen as a playful approach that uses artistic means for reconnecting culture with ecologies. Using artistic and creative modes of modeling, one can shift focus, participate in, and become a source of meanings for the rest of the ecosystem. The final subsection provides an example of such a creative approach in which the image of the forest has been adopted as the ground for semiotic modeling.

Semiotics, especially as it is developed in the ecosemiotic paradigm, appears to offer new and unused capacities for environmental humanities. This potential springs from basic semiotic concepts and tools that allow connecting, relating, and integrating phenomena that are usually treated as belonging to different ontological domains or to subjects of different disciplines. For instance, the sign concept itself is well suited to a semiotic interpretation of ecological issues. Sign as developed in the semiotics of Charles S. Peirce (CP 1931–56) can be understood as a mediator, a connector between the various aspects of the world. The Peircean sign is tripartite: a connecting sign in a narrow sense (representamen); the object of the sign; and its interpretation (interpretant), while these parts can belong to different mental, textual, and physical realms. The sign – or, more precisely semiosis, that is the sign's processual manifestation – allows some sort of connection to emerge that otherwise would be nonexisting. As such, signs can glue together various entities and beings of the world into meaningful relations, thus embodying a huge ecological potential to reconnect, to heal.

Ecosemiotics is not a modernist or structuralist approach; nor does it belong to the postmodern schools of cultural studies and literary criticism (as it has developed from the 1960s onward). In line with the thought of British semioticians Paul Cobley (2016) and Wendy Wheeler (2016) on biosemiotics, ecosemiotics can be described as belonging to a third way of thinking that seeks to contextualize semiotic processes and creative freedom within the constraints and hard realities of the earth. Cultural creativity and material realities are not seen here as excluding or conflicting with one another, but rather their encounters are the very condition for the meanings and significance to unfold. This idea was entitled *Expecting the Earth* by Wendy Wheeler (2016) as an observation that we as well as all other biological organisms have innate cognitive and semiotic readiness to meet the earthly patterns and processes. We anticipate encountering the earth in its various forms but do so inventively and playfully. The focus of ecosemiotics is thus on the interactions between environmental conditions and semiotic processes and the diversity of life stories, meaning-making strategies, and narratives that spring from these intertwinings. Such an approach can perhaps be labeled the "ecological postmodern" as was proposed by Charlene Spretnak (1997) who characterized it as aiming at a plurality in contexts. Ecosemiotics builds its argumentation on the excluded middle and interplays between culture and the ecosystem, humans and other animals, signs and matter, freedom and causality.

1 Signs In Ecology

1.1 Organisms' Relations with the Environment are Based on Signs

A few years ago, I witnessed a European robin *Erithacus rubecula* wintering in a large shopping mall near my home town. In Estonia, winters are normally too harsh for insectivorous birds; so robins stay and nest there just during summers. One bird, however, had discovered a warm refuge in a commercial center that kept her from leaving in the autumn. She wintered, and I believe successfully, in a novel environment with which she previously had no evolutionary or individual experience. During that winter, she, no doubt, needed to solve a number of practical issues, such as navigating in the artificial habitat, finding the right type of food and drinking water, finding shelter from curious people and cleaning machines, and so forth. She needed to use all her wit to combine her bodily and cognitive capacities with this new environment and find workable solutions.

Now, the impact of human action on natural environments has turned the latter increasingly more unpredictable and unstable for other species. Metaphorically speaking, we are turning the entire world into a large shopping mall. What helps us understand the survival of other species in these shifting and changing environments is not fixed behavioral patterns and the struggle for survival, but approaches that connect animals and the environment by dynamical processes such as recognition, affordances, semiosis, and abduction. In most of twentieth-century biology, relations between animals and their environment have been seen in terms of rigid oppositions, while the role of animal subjects themselves has been considered quite minimal. Comparative psychology and classic ethology comprehended animals as sets of predispositions to react to the environment's stimuli in fixed ways. This understanding finds clear expression in the vocabulary of mid-twentieth-century animal biology: stimulus; releaser; instinct; fixed action pattern; and imprinting. The later evolutionist schools of animal behavior (sociobiology, behavioral ecology) understood animals mainly as executors of their genetic programs, competing against one another for environmental resources. From an ecosemiotic view, the main problem with these twentieth-century paradigms is their underlying presumption that the animal and the environment are two distinct and fixed entities. Mostly, this is not the case.

Animals using semiosis or mediated relations to make sense of the environment is a phenomenon so widely present that it is very easily overlooked. Let us recall that, for an animal, a sign is anything that indicates, shows the way, or makes evident something that would otherwise remain concealed or inaccessible. Even if we skip the philosophical question whether all perceptions of environmental objects are mediated by our senses and thus semiosic, we will find animals relying on mediated relations everywhere. A huge number of predatory species from snakes and sharks to big cats use smell or tracks to trace down the location of their prey. Many animals – fish, insects, birds, and mammals – rely in their movement and migration on various types of environmental signs: memorized landmarks; stellar constellations; chemical traces in air and water; and so on. Many birds gather and synthesize different qualities of the environment to decide on where to build their nest. Habitat preference is semiosic as it includes generalization, and generalizations cannot be made on the level of particulars but need semiotic mediation.

In semiotic terminology, sign relations between animals and their environmental entities are often *indexes* where the connection between the sign and the object the sign refers to is based on some form of causal effect, correlation, or spatial relation between the two. This is the case in many natural signs (e.g. smoke signifying fire) as opposed to conventional signs that are intentionally conveyed in human language (Nöth 2001). Often such signs also have metric or metered qualities, that is, the scope or reach of the sign can be used as a measure to determine the quality or quantity of the related object (Farina 2008). We can think here about the size or brightness of flower blossoms signaling the quantity or sugar content of the nectar to bees and other pollinators. The sign relations between the animal and the environment can be further described and classified based on various criteria: the type of relationship between the sign and the object; the accessibility of the sign relations to the animal; the abstractness of the sign (see further, Maran 2017b). The astounding number and diversity of environmental signs defies reduction; that is, environmental signs cannot be viewed solely as projections of an organism's cognition to the environment nor can they be approached as objective properties of the environment. Rather, environmental signs appear where the qualities of the environment and the animal's meaning-making activities meet.

Broader foundations for the ecosemiotic model of approaching these subtle relations can be found in the works of German-Baltic (Estonian) biologist Jakob von Uexküll, who, in the early twentieth century, developed a view in theoretical biology that was based on relations and meanings (Uexküll 1982). One of his central concepts was *Umwelt*, understood as a subjective perception of the world where animal interacted with the surrounding environment through species-specific senses and activities. In Uexküll's view, each *Umwelt* is organized by central meanings and through the *Umwelt* each species perceives the world in a distinctive way, even if the species inhabited the very same physical environment. More specifically, the relationship between the animal and the environmental object could be broken down to an array of intermediate stages: sense organs, cues and cue carriers that together with the animal's activity toward the same environmental object, formed a cycle of interaction (the functional cycle or *Funktionskreis* in Uexküll's terminology). The *Umwelt* concept is also applicable to the human species. Differently from other animals, human perception of the world is largely organized by categories and distinctions taking place in the internal world (*Innenwelt*).

As described earlier, for ecosemiotics an important part of this relationship consists in the properties and patterns of the environment – what resources and perceptually accessible qualities the given environment provides to which the animal can relate. This potential of the environment is sometimes called *perceptual affordance* following the works of psychologist James J. Gibson (1979: 127ff). An environment can afford support, shelter, food, nesting place, and so on to an animal, and as animal *Umwelten* differ, the same environment can afford different things to different species. Including affordances and resources in the research model allows us to describe and compare semiotic potentials and qualities of the environments by relying on the perspectives and judgments of the inhabitants of these environments. This in its turn gives a solid ground for arguing about the quality and intrinsic value of the environment – an issue that appears to be problematic for many postmodern paradigms.[1] There is also the practical method of *Ecological Repertoire Analysis* that focuses on local heterogeny and semiotic relations that nonhuman species have with the environment (Maran 2020b). For instance, we can analyze how the meanings and affordances of the environment have impoverished for other species when comparing the situations before and after human intervention.

We could also adopt a broader and more structured approach and describe, in the common framework, patterns of animal *Umwelten* and environmental properties. A possibility for articulating the animal–environment relationship spatially was proposed by Italian landscape ecologist Almo Farina (2006; Farina and Belgrano 2004, 2006) in his original research framework of *ecofields*. Farina talks about the need–function–ecofield (or interface)–resource sequence (Farina 2012: 23), where needs are basic biological necessities that an organism has, functions are behavioral motivations that make it possible for an animal to relate with an environment in certain ways, whereas resources allow animals to fulfill their biological needs. The ecofield in Farina's vocabulary is a meeting point of an animal's biological requirements on the one hand, and the properties and resources of the landscape on the other. "The term ecofield is the contraction of the words 'ecological field', and means the physical (ecological) space and the associated abiotic and biotic characters that are perceived by a species when a functional trait is active" (Farina and Belgrano 2004: 108). If a behavioral function of the animal meets a suitable location in the environment, this location or patch becomes actualized as an ecofield. Functions and resources are therefore necessarily mediated by a semiotic component – the ecofield (interface) – that an animal needs to perceive and interpret correctly to make use of a resource.

For instance, an interface standing for drinking water may be the perception of a reflecting surface. Animals interpret the interface in order to gain access to related resources, but as a semiotic process this relationship is probable – an animal may also have inadequate competence to reach the interpretation or the interface may give a false premise about the resource. At this point we may

---

[1] A view that integrates life and matter, human and animals, the subjective and the objective, can also serve as a basis for an ecosemiotic definition of the environment. In this text, environment is understood as a complex phenomenon that has three characteristics: "environment: (1) includes multitudes of *Umwelten* of organisms of different species and interactions between them; (2) contains physical forces, structures, and resources that can be objects of interpretation, that can constrain interpretation or be a context for interpretation; (3) provides conditions for the multisensory and multilayered semiosis from tactile to symbol-based semiosis" (Maran 2017b: 356).

think about human-made surfaces such as asphalt or sheet metal that lure diving beetles *Dytiscus* with their reflection, yet do not offer the pond or creek habitat that the insect is looking for. A possibility for misinterpretation proves that we are dealing with semiotic phenomena, as, according to Umberto Eco, "semiotics is in principle the discipline studying everything which can be used in order to lie" (Eco 1976: 7). Farina's ecosemiotic approach is also very suitable for analyzing cases in which normal sequences of need–function–ecofield–resource do not work and animals are not able to use signs accessible to them to find resources that they need. This may often be the case in semi-natural, urban, and technical environments, where the human impact is large.

Focusing on the animal–environment relationship will change the way eco-semiotics sees specific places or landscapes. Instead of approaching these objectively through measurements and geographies or, alternatively, taking these as human cultural constructions, ecosemiotics offers a third way of understanding landscapes. In an ecosemiotic view, the land area becomes a composition of various environmental resources and affordances with a number of perceivable interfaces and a variety of species that relate with the habitat based on their biological organization and needs. As Almo Farina and Nadia Pieretti have put it, "a landscape is not only a geographical entity but also a cognitive medium. The landscape may be considered a semiotic context used by the organisms to locate resources heterogeneously distributed in space and time" (Farina and Pieretti 2013: 1). A similar approach is adopted by Hans Van Dyck (2012) in his "functional landscape" with applications to species protec-tion and landscape restoration. Through an ecosemiotic lens the environment in its spatial constitution becomes a matrix of qualitative meaning connections between animals and the land.

In past decades biology has developed in a direction more favorable to eco- and biosemiotic views. What has changed in particular, is the understanding of the role that the environment has in organisms' development, while the two are increasingly less considered as radically distinct categories (West-Eberhard 2003). This has largely to do with better knowledge of epigenetic factors as individual or environmental properties that influence the manifestation of genes and related phenomena of polyphenism, reaction norms, etc. Evolutionary developmental biology, and especially ecological developmental biology as developed by Scott Gilbert (Gilbert and Epel 2008), has demonstrated the role of environmental factors in early individual development of animal species. Temperature influencing the sex determination in reptiles, the presence of natural predators in water causing crustaceans *Daphnia* to select different developmental tracks and develop a large protective crest, the presence of gut microbiota as linked to the development of the endocrine system in humans, are some examples of these complex relationships. A more semiotic interpretation of such interrelations is provided by Morten Tønnessen (2014) as a concept of *Umwelt trajectories* to indicate that animals in their relations with the environment are dynamically shifting from one stage to another, forming a trajectory of changing world-schemas. Danish biosemiotician Jesper Hoffmeyer (2008) has further described the active role that an animal with its various semiotic competences has in creating a correspondence between its own genetic and bodily information and environmental information. In Hoffmeyer's view, matching an animal's genetic heritage with the conditions of the surrounding environment is an active and dynamic semiotic process similar to the human process of translating between different languages.

The ever-changing relations between an animal and the environment are not relations between distinct entities, but what is changing is rather the semiotically active and intertwined complex of organism plus the environment. The diversity of environmental conditions and micro-environments challenge animals for cognitive plasticity, as they have to learn and adapt to the changing local conditions. Even such a simple task as a bird looking for an insect in the foliage is actually a complex puzzle because of the changing light conditions, the variety of shapes of leaves and branches, the movement of wind, and so on. Behavioral ecologists Lyndon A. Jordan and Michael J. Ryan (2015) have argued that in complex environments, behavioral plasticity depends on the animal's ability to integrate numerous sensory stimuli and, to understand this process, the animal's own perceptual space or *Umwelt* needs to be brought into a central focus. Under such conditions, the animal *Umwelt* can be seen as a focal point, where different sources of information are put together, where interpretation and choices are made.

When looking for such correspondence between itself and the environment, the animal has different possibilities: its own biological structure can change (as demonstrated by developmental biology); it can change its location and involvement in the environment by interpretation and active behaviors (such as migration or habitat selection); or it can actively change the environment for the environment to become more suitable for itself. The latter option is known under the label of *niche construction* (Odling-Smee et al. 2003; Peterson et al. 2018): animals' changing of their ecological niches to make these more suitable for themselves: "Niche construction involves reciprocal responses between organisms and the biota (and abiota) comprising their surrounding environment. When organisms respond to environmental pressures the environment itself can be modified and a feedback mechanism may be created and later canalized" (Peterson et al. 2018: 183). Niche construction may be passive as just a byproduct of living processes or actions, e.g. animals making paths in landscapes simply by moving across them, or it can be the result of more intentional activities such as nest building of collective Hymenopteras (wasps, bees, bumblebees). By constructing their niches, various species create conditions in which they benefit more from the flows of matter and energy (e.g. creating a more stable microclimate, storing food), etc.

From an ecosemiotic perspective, the result of niche construction is that animals and the environment become even more intertwined and the boundaries between them blurred. Through intentional alteration of the environment, an animal becomes *rooted* in the environment both energetically and semiotically. Orb-weaving spiders serve as a vivid and often-used example. Uexküll (1982) gave the spider as an example of the plan-based structure of nature, but from an ecosemiotic perspective we may also ask if there is any reasonable way to determine the borders that separate the spider from its environment. The silk that the spider produces is its bodily secretion, thus, by its chemical constitution very much what the spider is. Without the silk, orb-weaving spiders would not be able to feed. Still, the spider's web becomes functional only if carefully positioned between straws, branches, or other environmental objects and taking into account open flyways and the movement of insects. The combination of glued and glueless silk needs to suit the local micro-topology, as well as the spider's own needs and movement possibilities. In this sense, the surrounding straws and branches also become a part of what the spider is. In weaving the web the spider takes into account and combines all these different sources of information. We can thus describe different connection zones and thresholds, but, from a semiotic perspective, it becomes extremely difficult to draw any fixed border between the animal and the environment. What glues an animal and the environment together is the meaning relations, semiosis.

Animals' ability to cope with the changing ecologies of the contemporary times (spread of urban environments, anthropogenic changes in interspecies relations, shifting boundaries of seasons, extreme weather events, etc.) largely depends on the plasticity or rigidity of the semiotic relations that they have with the environment. For instance, if the abundance of prey species diminishes quickly, will a predator be capable of finding and developing a novel image of prey as has been noticed in black-footed ferrets in regard to the declining prey populations of prairie dogs (Candland 2005)? In other cases, animals' semiotic relations with the environment can be intentionally used by humans to create new habits in animals as reported by Van Dyck (2012) on the experiments made with orange-tip butterflies *Anthocharis cardamines*. In this study, regular host plants of the butterfly were planted outside the limits of their regular habitats to invite the butterfly to new locations. From an ecosemiotic perspective the important question is what the possibilities are for adjusting semiotic relations in the face of environmental change and how, in the changing world, to find semiotic practices that are more sustainable and durable in the long run, both for humans and for other animals. The solutions appear in developing a better understanding of processes that can be used to establish new semiotic relations, either through adaptive play-like processes or through semiotic modeling that helps to build new associations.

1.2 Communication is a Foundation of Ecological Relations

The ideal model object for semiotics has been human language; also historically, semiotics as a discipline has been largely developed within language studies with some inputs from medicine, theology, and philosophy. However, humans are definitely not the only species capable of communication or boasting a complex species-specific communication system. Most vertebrates as well as insects, and especially species with complex social relations, use diverse means of communication to convey information about their presence, needs, interests, and surrounding conditions. Messages can be communicated through various media such as smell, sound, touch, gestures, and movement, and they can be temporally organized into more complex messages. Although the sign systems of other species are simpler than human language (especially as regards their syntactic and referential capacities), they have been shown to be capable of conveying complex information. Classic studies by Karl von Frisch showed how by their so-called waggle dance – circular dance-like movements made on the honeycomb – honey bees can exchange information about the distance and direction of the nectar sources. A number of bird species have been shown to have combinatorial properties in their alarm calls that allow the birds to differentiate between different types of predators or between predators and brood parasites (e.g. in Suzuki 2016). Peter Marler, Thomas A. Sebeok, Jack P. Hailman, Dario Martinelli, and other scholars of semiotics of animal communication (or zoosemiotics) have demonstrated that semiotic concepts (such as code, reference, context, lexicon, and others) work well in analyzing forms of animal communication. In a broader perspective, this means that animals use mediated information to regulate the various aspects of their lives such as social hierarchies, population densities, relations with offspring, and collective behavior.

Why does it matter if animals relate and respond to the changes of one another's behavior mechanically, or whether they actively convey and interpret signs in communication? Mechanical relations require a direct immediate relationship and precise matching between the participants as is the case with a matching key and padlock. In nature, such situations may arise, especially in biochemical processes in which chemical affinities and structural matches count, or at the organismal level in situations, or where recognition occurs based on simple physical compatibility. On the organismal level, the species-specific matching of reproductive organs of males and females could be considered as an example of such mechanical relationship that effectively limits hybridization. Sign-based communication, however, has properties that make it possible to organize groups of living organisms in very different ways. Communication is *mediated*, which means that it allows regulating relations over spatial and temporal distances. This mediatedness makes it possible to use sounds and smells to convey information on how tensely a given environment is populated and by whom. Communication is *agential*, which means that it involves specific agents that make communication happen based on their *Umwelten*, subjective perceptions, experiences, and competencies. As such, communication can be seen as a translation device that creates links and makes transmissions between an animal's internal needs, motivations, and preferences, and the external conditions and resources. Communication is also *open*, which means that in most cases messages are transmitted in some medium (vibrations, colors, chemical compounds) that is accessible to third counterparts. This makes possible all sorts of secondary relations such as eavesdropping, where information is made use of by subjects for whom it was not originally intended. The openness of communication allows building inter-species communication networks and, in connection with this, various forms of mutualistic relations (e.g. Tobias et al. 2014). The openness of such communication networks embraces also humans who can use animal vocalizations, sounds, and smells to relate to and make sense of biological communities. Treating communication in nature as mediated, agential, and open allows us to understand how it connects, integrates, and makes regulation between animals within and between species possible.

Animal communication systems contain signs and meanings that can be easily interpreted and incorporated in the semiotic activities of other species. Features of organisms that have to do with the communicative function have the potential to become integrated in new semiotic relations, where they are often endowed with new meanings. Kleisner and I have called such readiness of the shape or structure to obtain meaning based on some earlier semiotic relations *semiotic cooption* (Maran and Kleisner 2010). An example of this can be the phenomenon that other species living in the same environment tend to interpret any symmetrical and round spots on animal surfaces as eyes. This peculiarity is a basis of diversity and abundance of eye spots that are usually used to deter predators, and thus constitute part of warning displays. A related idea has been proposed by Jesper Hoffmeyer as *semethic interaction*. This strange-sounding term refers to the observation that, in living organisms, existing patterns, structures, and routines tend to become sources of interpretation: "Whenever a regular behavior or habit of an individual or species is interpreted as a sign by some other individuals (conspecific or alter-specific) and is reacted upon through the release of yet other regular behaviors or habits, we have a case of semethic interaction" (Hoffmeyer 2008: 189). The idea of semethic interaction is based on Hoffmeyer's earlier observation that new habits in nature tend to become signs for some other parties living in the environment (Emmeche et al. 2002: 20).

Thus, nature tends to acquire habits and these habits tend to gain semiotic quality and meaning either in new or existing ecological relations. What often follows is the kind of meaning cascades that interconnect many species in a given ecosystem. For instance, blossoms of daisies, dandelions, and other plants transmit messages about the presence of nectar and pollen to flies, hoverflies, butterflies, and many other insects. The habit of pollinators to visit colorful plants is in turn used by crab spiders *Thomisidae*, who wait and lurk in blossoms and have a special ability of adjusting their body colors to the respective flower. The crab spiders' habit of sitting in the blossoms is made use of by parasitic mud dauber wasps *Sceliphron sp.*, many species of which are specialized in catching spiders. They will look for spiders in the flowers, paralyze them, and transport them into their nests where they inject eggs into the spiders to turn them into food for the developing wasp larvae. Thus the cascades of linkages between habits, signs, recognition, and adaptation may connect a number of species in the ecosystem with one another. We can see that ecological relations and food webs are largely present due to the participants' abilities in perceiving, recognizing, and memorizing one another, but also due to their abilities to communicate their identity, intentions, location, and surrounding resources.

Another important possibility for animals to become interrelated via communication has to do with overlaps in communication media. Animals, whether they belong to the same species or to different ones, use the same channels or media and this creates a ground for mutually shared messages. Animals may also use the physical environment as a medium for exchanging messages, as the traces of their activities in the environment have sign value. Bears mark their territory by making claw-marks on trees; canines and mustelids often leave their excrements on stones, fallen trees, and other higher spots in the landscape; traces of life activities such as beaver dams, food-harvesting sites of woodpeckers, etc., signal the presence of the animals in the habitat. Russian ethologist and semiotician Elina Vladimirova (2009) has demonstrated how some species (e.g. red foxes) spend much time following and reading the marks that have been left in the environment by other species. Here the environmental structures become something of a memory tool or recording device to save and mediate information about the presence and activities of various species.

When different species communicate via the same medium or channel, the message exchanges between them may also interfere with and obstruct one another. Birds have been shown to use sound frequencies for communication that are less covered by the noise elicited by living or physical sources such as the high-pitch vocalizations of amphibians in the tropics or the low noise of waves and wind in coastal areas, respectively (Bradbury and Vehrencamp 2011: 81). This is the reason why gulls living in urban areas use high-pitched cries that may be rather irritating to human ears. Various examples of mimicry and camouflage demonstrate how species have become adapted to using the same channels for communication in situations in which they have contradictory needs and intensions (Maran 2017a). In such cases, animals often need to balance their different needs, e.g. use vivid color signals to attract a mate, but at the same time use camouflage to hide from potential predators. Human technological activities often use the same communication channels as other species and therefore can obstruct their communication as well. Traffic noise is known to mask vocal communication of songbirds, and light pollution seriously hinders the navigating of many nocturnal species (e.g. moths, sea turtles). Humans' negative effects on other species and also ecosystems are often not caused by physical destruction, but are due to their obstructing and interfering with intra- and interspecies semiotic relations (cf. Slabbekoorn and Halfwerk 2009). To conclude, communication networks in ecosystems are complex and open for humans to make sense of and participate in. Nature is semiotically open to culture and has always been so. It was we humans who turned away from it and, largely with religious, philosophical, and ideological motivation, have denied voice and meaning to nature.

1.3 Semiosis Regulates Ecosystems

So far, we have observed various examples of meaning-making in organisms' relations with their environments, as well as between different organisms. However, it is much more difficult to claim something conclusive about the role of semiosis on the level of the ecosystem. The main reason for this is the lack of research on the topic, which has largely been caused by how ecology has been developing as a science. There have been two dominant schools in ecology: population ecology; and ecosystem ecology. Population ecology has first and foremost been interested in demographics, influencing factors, and evolutionary dynamics of single or a few species. This may have drawn attention to apparently semiotic aspects such as food preference or mate choice, but this interest has seldom reached the discussion of the higher organizational layers of ecological systems. Ecosystem ecology, on the other hand, has paid much attention to the flows of energy and matter in ecosystems and has developed complex mathematical methods to study this large-scale structure (that is, pools, flows, trophic levels, bioproduction, etc.) of the ecosystems (Jørgensen 1992; Hagen 1992). On this scale of generalization, the semiotic activity of organisms as well as the dynamics of populations is usually considered as a variation below statistical relevance.

Nevertheless, there are some ideas and research in ecology that may point at the role of semiotic processes also in ecosystem regulation. Given the depth and broad reach of ecosystem studies, only a very brief introduction to ecosystem functioning can be given here. First, it would be important to grasp the number and role of ecological relations in ecosystems. Jørgensen and Müller (2000: 5) estimate that, depending on the ecosystem, the number of species involved may range from 1,000 to 100,000. At the same time, ecosystems that persist under extreme climate conditions or are affected by pollution may be stable at a much lower species count (Woodward 1994). It is not easy to determine the number of ecological relations that connect the species. Relations in ecosystems differ in their intensity: some are essential for the very functioning of the ecosystem (around the so-called keystone species), others occasional or weak. Therefore, the very task of determining the number of ecological relations is somewhat arbitrary and related to the issue of where to draw the threshold.

There is also a debate going on in ecology on the relationship between the number of species in the ecosystem and the number of linkages connecting the species. Some scholars have shown that the number of linkages grows exponentially in regard to species count, whereas others claim that the ratio between the species count and the number of linkages remains relatively constant due to balancing factors (e.g. larger ecosystems are more heterogenic, species specialize, etc.). As a rough simplification, it can be claimed on the basis of several studies of actual food webs that the number of linkages (trophic interactions) is about ten times higher than the species count in an ecosystem. For instance, in the arctic marine ecosystem the number of ecological relations per species ranged from 6 to 13 (de Santana et al. 2013). In a study made by Laigle et al. (2018) in Germany on soil invertebrate communities the food web was found to contain between 89 and 168 species, whereas the number of trophic interactions ranged from 729 to 3,344. In general, species in ecological systems seem to be very well connected through different types of linkages and this provides a solid condition for semiosis-based regulation in ecosystems.

A basic framework for understanding the semiotic regulation of ecosystems consists of three interrelated parts: (1) material or energetic constraints that restrict the number of possibilities (resources, habitats, environment); (2) a degree of autonomy of individual organisms to act and react in regard to the surroundings (organismal self-regulation, closure, metabolism); (3) semiotic capacities of perception, recognition, learning, and memory, which make it possible to relate material constraints and actions, but do this in a number of different ways. These components of semiotic regulation are engaged in each and every ecological relation from symbiosis and commensalism to parasitism and predation.

In direct trophic interactions such as predation the semiotic regulation is evident in the processes of prey recognition, of applying suitable hunting strategy, of adaptations in order to notice and avoid predators, etc. At the same time, also, indirect and mild ecological interactions may involve important semiotic input. A type of such indirect interaction is facilitation (or facultative mutualism). In case of facilitation, at least one species creates suitable conditions for the other species and the relationship is not harmful for either. A facilitation may occur for instance by eliminating competitors or deterring predators or through reducing thermal, water, or nutrient stress via shading or through nutritional symbioses (Bruno et al. 2003: 120; Stachowicz 2001: 235). The relevance of indirect ecological relationships, such as facilitation of the regulation of the ecosystem, lies in the fact that even the simple thriving of a species – which may be regulated by semiotic relations and communication within the species (as described in Section 1.2) – can have effects on other species and thus on the broader biological community. The abundance of mild and indirect facilitation relationships is much higher compared to what are usually considered as trophic interactions in ecosystems.

The role of semiotic processes in the regulation of biological communities becomes clearer in observing interspecies communication networks. Goodale and colleagues (2010) describe various ways in which interspecies information transfer can have an effect on community structures. Often, grouping and communication occurs between the members of different species as their different perception of the world allows them to share more effectively information about resources and predators. Interspecies communication can also have more long-lasting effects as animals may select their habitats based on cues and messages received from other species; migration routes may be chosen based on information received from other species; or interspecies communication may be part of regulating population densities. A relatively well-studied phenomenon among such examples is the regulatory function of vocal communication of passerine birds. Malavasi and her colleagues (2014) argue that birds' singing often establishes cross-species conventions that the authors call acoustic codes, and that these conventions allow birds themselves to regulate their density in biological communities. By listening, adapting, and tuning in to the morning chorus, individual birds receive information about the crowdedness of the habitat and location of unoccupied areas and resources.

Another process in which the organisms themselves select and adjust their location and relations with the resources, species mates, and other species within the ecosystem, has been called *ecological fitting* (Janzen 1985). The idea behind this concept is that species' coexistence in biological communities does not usually result from long-term coevolution of the species, but a result from more rapid processes of behavioral choice. Animals find their place in an ecosystem by actively looking for a location where their needs would be best met and their physiological and behavioral qualities would best suit the surrounding conditions. An example of such a fitting process can be habitat preference based on risk assessments that animals undertake concerning the presence of predators (such environment descriptions have been called *landscapes of fear*, Bleicher 2017). On the level of the species, ecological fitting becomes an effective mechanism for forming aggregations between different species. By looking for, and finding, a good spot to inhabit, individuals belonging to various species are, in fact, creating the composition of the ecosystem. The concept of ecological fitting was originally used to explain high biodiversity in tropical ecosystems, but the same mechanism appears to be present in other ecosystems as well (Agosta and Klemens 2008). At the same time, aggregation due to ecological fitting may become an important factor of the subsequent ecosystem regulation and evolution, as such species aggregations form the further context and conditions in which the species will live. In such a case, semiosis may become an essential factor in evolution.

In such examples we have, in principle, local feedback cycles in which meaning-making – emitting, receiving, recognizing, and interpreting messages – enables animals to regulate flows of energy and matter in a particular spot of the ecosystem. System ecologists Bernhard Patten and Eugene Odum (1981) have argued that this informational layer comprising an enormous number of local feedback cycles is the main reason why ecosystems retain their relatively stable structure and do not disperse into myriads of chaotic events. They further describe informational processes that allow connecting different entities and layers of the ecosystem as mapping – which corresponds to iconic signs in the semiotic jargon – and amplification, in which a small causal trigger can have a major output effect due to semiotic mediation. The amplification effect can be illustrated by herbivorous insects such as bark beetles (Raffa et al. 2008). In most cases the damaging effect of the bark beetles

Scolytinae to conifer forests is spatially restricted as the activities of the insects and the defense mechanisms of pines are well balanced with one another.[2] If, however, the defense mechanisms (the tree's ability to signal an attack, increased resin production, increased protective chemical in resin) are decreased due to physiological stresses (climate warming, anthropogenic pollution), then large-scale bark-beetle invasions may occur easily.

This semiotic regulatory layer of the ecosystem has been termed as an information network (Patten and Odum 1981) or communication network (Lévêque 2003: 95). Danish system scientist Søren N. Nielsen (2007) has rightly recognized the semiotic character of this layer and proposed that it should be called "semiotype" in parallel to "genotype" and "phenotype." Using the example of bees and pollination, he precisely describes the cumulative nature of this semiotic layer (Nielsen 2007: 99):

> It may be worth trying to describe ecosystem semiotics on a more macroscopic level and explain that they are somehow mandatory and crucial to proper ecosystem function. We may do that in several "Gedankenexperiments". As an example, one may put the question: Where would ecosystems be without insects to pollinate flowers? – a question commonly raised when discussing ecosystem services. But we tend to ignore that the proper function of insects in this context is highly dependent on a proper semiotic function of the system. Bees could hypothetically be flying around in a random manner – which indeed would most likely lead to the result that some flowers would be fertilised. But adding their ability to smell flowers, see them at distance, possibly remembering a good spot and for sure to communicate it to the "comrade workers" of the beehive would increase the probability for this. These semiotic processes are crucial not only to the beehive but also to the ecosystem as such.

The semiotic regulation in the ecosystem is indeed contextual and cumulative; it includes and combines patterns and perceivable properties of the inanimate environment, perception, interpretation, and behavioral action of single organisms, together with their memory, experience, and evolutionary past as well as communication networks in and between species. These numerous tiny acts of meaning-making organize and regulate the ecosystem in its every joint and connection, forming a complex multilayered network (Nielsen 2016). Being qualitative by nature, that is, based on qualities, feelings and recognition, the semiotic regulation of ecosystems constitutes a whole that is very difficult to rationalize by using scientific methods. Nevertheless, this semiotic regulation is

---

[2] This balance is achieved by active collective involvement of trees. Sánchez-García et al. (2017: 64) use the concept of *odortope* to indicate the "the non-random coordinated distribution of the odors in a forest," that mediates information about the condition of trees, activities of bark beetles, as well as parasitic and predatory insects.

very real as we find out through bitter experiences, when disturbance in communication causes severe malfunction in ecosystems. It is not an exaggeration to claim that the natural environment is essentially meaningful, and not only for humans; rather, we could say that the ecological system itself is endowed with meanings.

2 Nature In Culture

2.1 Criticism of Purely Symbolic Culture

Let me start this section with a tale on fishing. *A boy sits on a riverbank catching fish, but has used up all his worms. However, he quickly figures out a solution by taking a pen and writing "WORM" on a piece of paper. The boy then puts the paper on the hook and continues fishing as if nothing had changed. It does not take long until the float disappears under the water. The boy pulls excitedly to find a larger piece of paper attached to the hook. "EEL" has been written on the paper in rough letters.* This funny story can be interpreted as a distorted version of Adam's task of naming animals, in which symbolic language is used outside of its expected context in the natural environment. Yet, unexpectedly, nature responds to the human linguistic activity using the same mode of expression, for the boy only to discover that there is nothing he can do with a piece of paper with letters E-E-L on it. The letters are not the same as the fish and cannot be eaten. So the fishing activity, which is originally human deception played out against the fish, becomes a double deception in which articulated language is used instead, only to be barred by counter-deception by an unknown underwater force. Or perhaps this joke should be rather interpreted as a fable about human self-deception in cases when we substitute our denominations of animals, landscapes, and natural resources for these, just to find out later that our conventional signs and cultural codes cannot be used as shelter against the elements, that they neither deliver warmth nor are good for eating.

Such hegemony of cultural symbols over ecosystems appears to be a rather widespread condition of our time as well as the root of many environmental problems. A central tenet of the modern worldview has been the belief that human culture is somehow superior to nature and independent from the ecosystem. This conviction manifests itself in a number of forms – viewing human language as a closed system of abstract formal relationships (as in the structuralism inspired by the linguistics of Ferdinand de Saussure); rejecting the possibility of direct relations between literary works and the extratextual environment; treating literature, music, performative, and fine arts as belonging to a high culture that is distant from any material everyday concerns, etc.

Criticisms of the modern worldview have already been launched from different angles by Bruno Latour, Donna Haraway, Karen Barad, Cary Wolfe, and other scholars of posthumanism, the Actor–Network theory, feminism, animal studies, and so on. There is no need to repeat these arguments here. My interest in the following pages is rather to shed light on the dynamics of cultural texts and systems that strive to become purely arbitrary and symbolic as well as on their effects upon ecosystems. Could it be that a culture whose ideal is to become self-sufficient itself poses an ecological threat, and if so, then what semiotic mechanisms are responsible for this and what are the possible solutions that semiotics could offer?

Let us first examine what it means to say that cultural entities (texts, discourses, and artefacts) are predominantly symbolic and what the problem with this symbolicity is. The idea of symbolic dominance is based on the semiotics of Charles S. Peirce. Symbol is one of many possible sign types that Peirce distinguishes in his complex typology of signs. Symbol is a sign in which the relationship between the sign in a narrow sense (representamen) and its object is conventional or arbitrary and is derived from cultural codes, social–cultural practices or habits typically associated with humans (which, however, may also be present in other social animal species). This means that differently from simpler sign types of icons and indexes, in symbols there is no motivated (causal or similarity-based) relation between the sign and its object. Typical examples of symbolic signs are human-language signs, in which the relation between the sound pattern and the idea it conveys is arbitrary as was pointed out already by the Swiss linguist Ferdinand de Saussure. This makes symbols autonomous or independent from their objects. For instance, the word "eel" does not have any causal or similarity-based connections with the particular fish species, and combinations of letters such as "anguilla," "aal," or "ugor" could suit the signifying purpose just as well.

The conventionality of symbolic signs has very important ecological consequences. Discourses, text, and artefacts that are purely symbolic or dominated by symbols are self-sufficient, in the sense that they can remain the same despite any changes on the object level. Or, alternatively, they can change and develop, driven by their own inner dynamics even if the object level remains the same. We saw above that both positive and negative feedback cycles are present (e.g. in symbiosis, predation) in ecosystems, making the system balanced in the long run. However, as they have no external reference or rooting, there is a deficit of negative feedback in symbol-based systems that would connect them to the object level. This is not the same as to say that symbol-based semiotic systems entirely lack negative feedback. There may be corrective feedback based on communicative codes, cultural regulation, and social norms. For instance, symbols that take part in communication can be understood or misunderstood. But on the level of the sign as a formal category, a feedback mechanism that interconnects signs with the object world is missing. Therefore, discourse, artefacts, and texts in culture that are predominantly symbolic can be repeated or reproduced to fill all the available media or to use up all the available resources. Overwhelming spread of tropes in social media and accelerating replacement of commodities with newer and newer goods can be seen as outcomes of this process.

The semiotic anthropology of Alf Hornborg (2001) analyzes the mechanics and effects of this symbolic hegemony, using the example of native South-American peoples (Amahuaca, Achuar, Huaorani, etc.). Departing from a number of case studies, he describes the primal semiotic activity of the indigenous peoples to be based on *sensory signs* that map the richness of the local horticulture through the sensations of eye, ear, nose, tongue, and skin that often have no linguistic equivalents. Sensory signs spread in the community through shared practices, imitation, and observation. Sensory signs are super-seded by *linguistic signs* that have been the main object of interest of anthro-pologists to understand ethnobiological classifications. Linguistic signs are, however, more standardized and limited compared to the sensory signs for distinguishing native plants and other entities of the ecosystem. The third category of signs in Hornborg's analysis are *economic signs* – these are signs whose value and meaning are separate from the object level and for this reason they can be used as means of exchange and markers of status and wealth. An absolute abstractness of economic signs is achieved in the Western understand-ing of currency that is an empty sign as it "can stand for anything to anybody" (Hornborg 1991: 156).

Economic signs make long-distance trade possible and, in relation to that, also enable production or accumulation of resources beyond one's needs and beyond the carrying capacity of the local ecosystem. In Hornborg's view, each subsequent sign type becomes more abstract and more detached from the human living practices in the ecosystem: Each of these semiotic levels is a prerequisite for the next, since linguistic signs must be mediated by sense organs and economic signs by cultural categories pertaining to exchange (e.g., "money", "price", "commodity", "wage"). On the other hand, each level has had a tendency to progressively detach itself from the logically and phylogenetically prior one, disembedding discourse from experience and economy from culture. (Hornborg 2001: 128)

Adoption of abstract sign systems becomes one of the main reasons for dismantling local cultures as Amerindian cosmologies rely on a particular perceptive of the world that is not consistent with the idea of semiotic generalization.[3] The value of Hornborg's study for this argumentation relies on demonstrating that there is a connection between specific types of sign systems and an emerging chasm between semiosis in culture and semiosis in the ecosystem.

However, the damaging effects of cultural entities dominated by symbols do not emerge only from their self-sufficiency and detachment from the ecosystems. To understand the destruction that the dominance of symbols brings along, we need to focus on the relationship between human semiotic resources (languages, texts, and discourses) and human action. Kalevi Kull (1998) has insightfully combined Jakob von Uexküll's functional cycle and culture–nature dynamics. If Uexküll's functional cycle (*Funktionskreis*) originally described the sign-mediated cycle of perception and action between the organism and the environmental object, then Kull applied this model to manifestations of nature in human culture. Humans perceive the environment based on their linguistic and cognitive abilities, filtering out what Kull calls *first nature*. For instance, they recognize herbs, berries, and mushrooms that they have names for. In the subsequent action toward the environment, humans depart from the distinctions that they have made, creating what is called *second nature* in Kull's terminology. For instance, we may pick berries we recognize and leave alone others we are not sure about. We may also draw a schematic map of a region and then decide our following actions based on the map and not on the actual environment. Often we actually do so. Thus, in culture–nature relations Uexküll's functional cycle becomes a machine that constantly prints the human touch and face upon nature and replaces natural communities with anthropogenic environments. As there is no empty place on the planet for a second nature, Kull's conclusion is rather pessimistic – the withdrawal of the wild and its replacement with a human-made environment is an inevitable outcome of human culture.

Uexküll's functional cycle of perception and action appears to be universal for the animal world as animals tend to change their environments to a certain degree according to their measure and meaning. Ants, beavers, and woodpeckers are capable of engineering their surroundings quite remarkably. We have also claimed that a similar process of imprinting one's own inner preferences and distinctions onto other organisms (both conspecific and other-specific) is widespread and present for instance in mimicry, sexual selection, and domestication (cf. *semiotic selection*; Maran and Kleisner 2010; also Maran 2014b). *Innenwelten* (that is Uexküll's term for the internal world) of animals tends to

---

[3] A similar view has been later developed by Eduardo Kohn: "Symbolic thought run wild can create minds radically separate from the indexical grounding their bodies might otherwise provide" (Kohn 2013: 49).

organize the *Umwelten* through action of other inhabitants of the same ecosystem. Acting based on one's own preference can also be considered a basic mechanism that animals use in niche construction. So, what is specific about humans and how does this relate to the devastating effects of the hegemony of symbols? In his analysis, Kalevi Kull (1998) brings out yet another type of nature, *third nature*, that he calls "image from image" or "model from model." This is an abstracted and purely artificial reflection of nature that appears in science and art (and, I might also add, in economics and politics). Being based on codes and sign systems of the respective media, the third nature has its endurance and agency. As Winfried Nöth (2014) has argued based on Peircean semiotics, symbols and symbol-based cultural artefacts are alive in the sense that they are autonomous, active, and purposeful. We can notice here similarity with Hornborg's economical signs that are also abstracted and distanced from the actual perception of nature. Examples of the dominance of third nature include organizing various plants according to the ideals of garden design, or taking the needs of the paper and pulp industry as the measure to determine the quantity of logging – basically all situations where the diversity of the living world is subordinated to abstracted values or measures. The endurance of symbols and their ability to induce habits give entities of third nature the capacity to shape human activities toward the ecosystem. What now becomes the critical question is: What do these *models from models* consist of and how are they constructed? Are they purely symbolic, or do they incorporate simpler iconic and indexical signs that still make relations with the object world possible? Are they homogeneous and univocal or rather places of dialogue that include different voices, some of which originate from the rest of the ecosystem? The impacts of different types of models in the culturenature cycle described by Kull are presumably very different. We will return to this question in the more detailed analysis of semiotic modeling in the third section.

However, the effects that the expansion of human symbol-based sign systems and their physical manifestations have on the rest of the ecosystem can be devastating. Human sign systems may overshadow the semiotic potential of the environment, hinder communicative activities of other species, and obstruct semiotic regulation in ecosystems. In his outstanding book *Malfeasance: Appropriation Through Pollution*, Michel Serres (2011: 70) paints a dystopic picture of human symbolic dominance: "On each mountain rock, each tree leaf, each agricultural plot of land, you have advertisements; letters are written on each blade of grass; the big name brands draw their giant images on the immense glaciers of the Himalaya. Like the legendary cathedral, the landscape is swallowed by the tsunami of signs." He continues: "Imperious images and letters force us to read, while the pleading things of the world are begging our senses for meaning. The latter ask; the former command. Our senses give meaning to the worlds; our products already have a meaning, which is flat" (Serres 2011: 50). Kull's cycle of different natures in the semiosphere describes how we replace the plurality of signs and meanings of numerous species and their manifestations in the ecosystem with semiotic activity of a single species – human. As a concrete illustration of such expansion of human symbols I would like to describe a campaign of regional tourism, "Life on the border of two worlds" that took place in the early 2000s in South Estonia. In cooperation with the National Geographic Corporation, the campaign aimed to promote local-nature tourism attractions and resulted in dozens of yellow window-like structures installed in picturesque locations. The rectangular steel and wood structures in a size taller than humans stand in a sharp contrast with the dynamics of the organic forms and pastel colors of surrounding bogs, hills, lakes, and forests. Natural landscapes change in diurnal and seasonal cycles with gusts of wind, varying light conditions, fog, and rain. Elks, wild boars, wolves, lynx, and other mammals come, go and interact with the environment and with one another. Migratory birds leave and return. Only the oversized yellow frames remain unchanging in contrast to living nature. There is no dynamics in them, no interaction with the surrounding, no other meaning except the visual representation of the corporate trademark.

Expansion of the human symbol-based sign to the ecosystem may bring along interruptive negative effects to other inhabitants of the ecosystem, which, following Ronald Posner (2000), can be called *semiotic pollution*. Posner draws our attention to the parallel between chemical contamination and semiotic pollution as both increase physiological stress in biological organisms. It takes additional energy and resources from various species to cope with excessive light signals produced by modern human civilization in the same way in which it is exhausting to deal with chemical pollutants contained in food or water. Semiotic pollution may disturb the code, contact, message, participants, and other aspects of the sign process. When the negative effects of human sign activities toward sign systems, semiotic activities, and meaningful landscapes of other species become too severe, we have reason to talk about extinction because of semiotic causes or *semiocide*. Estonian geologist and semiotician Ivar Puura (2013: 152) writes:

> The diversity of nature is overwhelming. Every living creature, being part of a greater whole, carries in itself memories of billions of years of evolution and embodies its own long and largely still unknown story of origin. By wholesale replacement of primeval nature with artificial environments, it is not only nature in the biological sense that is lost. At the hands of humans, millions of stories with billions of relations and variations perish. The rich signscape of

nature is replaced by something much poorer. It is not an exaggeration to call this process semiocide. I understand semiocide to be a situation in which signs and stories that are significant for someone are destroyed because of someone else's malevolence or carelessness, thereby stealing a part of the former's identity.

Deterioration of ecosystems is thus accompanied by semiocide and loss of signscapes for various animals that are processes much harder to detect. Let us try to sum up the argumentation in this point. Predominantly symbolic cultural entities are self-sufficient and closed. Their negative feedback is deficient and they have limited capacities for developing interactions with the object level of the environment or for dialogic relations with the other agencies in the ecosystems. Therefore, the hegemony of symbols has the tendency to bring along antagonism and semiocide. My aim here is not to develop crushing criticism against symbol-based human culture, even if this may seem so at first glance. Symbolic generalization and symbol-based modeling make possible scientific and artistic knowledge and thus acting toward the environment equipped with better knowledge and greater appreciation. The language that I am using in these very pages is also highly symbolic and abstract. What would need our attention, however, is the composition of cultural entities: to what extent they include simpler iconic and indexical sign relations; what their pragmatic involvement is in regard to the environment; and what possibilities their arrangements offer for the cultural entities to become related with the rest of the ecosystem.

2.2 Nonsymbolic Signs Connect Culture and the Ecosystem

Although symbolic-cultural systems appear to be closed and self-sufficient, it is actually not so. Culture has its autonomy, but it is partial and contextualized. As Bruno Latour (1993) famously declared, we have never achieved the ideal of fully ordered and systematic culture, *we have never been modern*. Relations between literary texts and social conditions have been well scrutinized by various critical disciplines such as culture studies, postcolonialism, feminism, and others. The contextual linkages between culture and ecosystems, however, have been addressed much less often. Following Jesper Hoffmeyer (1996: 95), there are two major directions we can focus at in this criticism. First, we can critically examine the semiotic processes that connect our conscious mind with the physiological processes of the body and through that the surrounding environment (which, according to Hoffmeyer, corresponds to psychosomatics). Or we can analyze different ways in which cultural texts and artefacts – poems, novels, theatrical performances, and movies – are in a direct contact with ecosystems through their representational capacities. These topics themselves are hardly new, but have been studied, for instance, in relation to the issues of embodiment and realism in literature. In the following pages, I hope to add some insights from semiotics by analyzing how and by which processes signs can connect culture and ecosystems.

Let us first address Hoffmeyer's field of the psychosomatic, that is, the question of how semiotic processes can connect the content of our minds with the physiological dynamics of our bodies. There is a wide range of research showing how our conscious thought does not take place in an isolated container, but is in a dynamic interrelation with the biochemistry of the body and even with other living organisms inside and around us. Neurobiologist Antonio Damásio (1994) has written about body-minded brain, claiming that the body provides a reference system that is essentially needed for the workings of a normal mind. He has also argued against the separation of thought and emotions, using various clinical cases to show that these are mostly interrelated. In brain studies, it is established that hormones (especially stress hormones such as cortisol and sex hormones such as estrogen) have a significant effect on human cognitive capacities (Lupien et al. 2007; Nielsen and Herrera 2017). In recent decades, extensive studies in the human microbiome have demonstrated that it is not only our physiology that affects cognition, but also changes in the bacterial populations that live inside us, which influence our mood, attention, and cognitive capacities. For instance, reduced gut microbiota appear to have a negative effect on the hippocampus (through exposure endotoxins and inflammation) with a related decline in cognitive function and mnemonic processes (Noble et al. 2017). Changes in gut microbiome are even likely to contribute to neurodegenerative diseases such as Alzheimer's and Parkinson's disease (Perlmutter 2019). Further, parasitic organisms may have an effect on human cognition: for instance, *Toxoplasma gondii*, a common parasite spread by cats, may affect dopamine-related regulation of motivation/reward and cognitive control in humans (Stock et al. 2017). Thus, conscious and logical thought of humans appears to be a rather special condition or abstraction, as in everyday situations cognition is immersed in our physiologies and fluctuates according to the availability of food, exposure to bacteria and parasites, and in the rhythm of changing physical conditions.

How, then, to analyze these psychosomatic linkages in semiotic terms in a way that would adequately describe the relationships between conscious thought and emotional physiological processes? In other words, how can we include our physiologies in semiotic models without reducing culture to chemical and physical processes as tends to happen in natural science? The best semiotic model for this that I can think of comes from the works of the Hungarian philosopher Michael Polanyi (1966). His concept of *tacit knowledge* is quite well known and broadly used in the fields of education and organization studies. Polanyi used tacit knowledge to explain various prelinguistic skills such as riding a bicycle, woodworking, face reading, and also the obtaining and transfer of these skills. It is less well known that Polanyi (1967; see also Gulick 2012) actually developed the concept of tacit knowledge in semiotic terms and proposed a detailed description of the constituents of such a sign model. In his view, the tacit sign has two poles or ends – the proximal and the distal end – and *from–to* structure. In the proximal end there are the miscellaneous processes that themselves are concealed from human attention and void of independent meaning.[4] The meaning arises through integration of these varied processes at the distal end of the sign relation. The proximal end acquires meaning retrospectively because of the established relationship between the individual entities: "We identified the two terms of tacit knowledge, the proximal and distal, and recognized the way we attend from the first to the second, thus achieving an integration of particulars to a coherent entity to which we are attending. Since we were not attending to the particulars in themselves, we could not identify them" (Polanyi 1966: 18). The sign model appears to be a precise description of various sensations and urges of the body of which we become aware only if a certain threshold has been crossed. As an example, we may think of a situation when a person needs to sit too long at his/her work desk as discomfort is growing and growing, and how it then crosses a certain invisible threshold and how then suddenly the awareness appears that the body has become stiff . . . that a leg is numb and that it is now certainly time to make a break in writing and take a short walk. Polanyi's tacit knowledge is a model that is able to describe such processes that pass the boundaries of our conscious mind and connect the mind and the body.

Tacit knowledge as a sign structure appears to be a move from the parts that are themselves meaningless to meaningful wholes. It expresses the integration of endosemiotic processes taking place in the hormonal, immunological, neural, and other semiotic systems of our bodies into cognitive content.[5] Tacit signs may be important for understanding how the environment influences our bodies to make an input into the cultural process and literary creation. In Polanyi's

---

[4] In Polanyi's philosophy, the proximal source of tacit knowledge is often hidden in participation in the world and this connects knowledge with personal experience, dwelling, and skill. Wendy Wheeler has called such a process of acquisition of knowledge the *semiotic knowledge*, pointing out that it springs from the streams of semiosis (Wheeler 2006: 63).

[5] Another conceptual possibility for integrating different semiotic processes of the human body was proposed by Thomas A. Sebeok as the notion of the *semiotic self*. According to Sebeok, the semiotic self is a multilayered structure, based on all memory-capable codes in the body (Sebeok 2001: 124) including at least immunological, neurological, cognitive, and, in the case of human animals, also verbal and narrative layers.

view, also higher linguistic and cultural capacities are based on tacit knowledge: "My view is that the use of language is a tacit performance; the meaning of language arises, as many other kinds of meaning do, in tacitly integrating hitherto meaningless acts into a bearing on a focus that thereby becomes their meaning" (Polanyi 1967: 315). Think here, for instance, how humans perceive sunshine. The physical environment and weather create preconditions in which the sun becomes perceptible to us. When our bodies are in the sun, many biochemical and physiological processes are launched in our organisms. The sun intensifies syntheses of melatonin in the pineal gland that regulates our mood and sexuality, of proclatine that regulates the sleep cycle, growth hormone that helps regeneration of cells and tissues, synthesis of vitamin D in the skin, and other biochemically active substances. On a neural level we perceive the sun as a tactile sensation of warmth on the skin and as a visual image reflected in our retina. We are probably not consciously aware of many of the physiological changes and biosemiotic processes going on in our bodies, yet tacit knowledge may become condensed in verbalization, knowledge, and even the linguistic description that the sun is something pleasant and positive. Finally, verse such as the following by Mary Oliver may be inspired by the bodily sensation of being in the sun: "do you think there is anywhere, in any language, / a word billowing enough / for the pleasure / that fills you / as the sun / reaches out, / as it warms you, / as you stand there / empty-handed" (Oliver 1992: 106). Each semiotic level of our bodies operates according to its own separate codes, regulations and integrations, but there are also semiotic processes between the different levels that connect the mind with emotions and language with the environment. Culture is not separate from our dwelling in the ecosystem.

Let us now observe the connection between culture and external nature that Jesper Hoffmeyer (1996: 95) called the environmental area. This raises the question of whether semiotic systems themselves that operate in culture can have a direct relationship with the environment, and if so, then how these relations can be described by semiotic models. The topic of closed semiotic systems in culture is a complex and lengthy philosophical discussion that can be demarcated by the historical aspiration toward ideal and contradiction-free artificial languages, formalist readings of literary works, structural linguistics, the apparatus of analytic philosophy to elaborate the clarity of thinking, and many other approaches. On the other hand, there are many schools of thought that have questioned the purity of language and cultural phenomena. In the 1980s, cognitive linguistics (Lakoff and Johnson 1980; 1999) critically addressed the conventionality of language by demonstrating the presence of conceptual metaphors – thought images deriving from the evolutionary experience of our ancestors. Approximately in the same period, cognitive ethology (Griffin 1976) and zoosemiotics (Sebeok 1990) developed tools for the theoretical analysis of animal communication that disrupted the separation between human language and communication systems of other species (for a discussion on their similarities and differences, see Maran 2010). Later works in distributed consciousness (Clark 1997) and distributed language studies (Cowley 2011) appeared to claim that for understanding language and consciousness it is essential to observe their functioning in real-life social situations, contexts, and dialogues. More recently, Arran Stibbe (2012; 2015) and others have advocated ecolinguistics as a critical approach in order to scrutinize the functioning of language in ecological crisis. These developments together have brought along a radical deviation from the thinking of language as a closed system and replaced this with understanding of the sign as a means of finding connections and participating in patterns of the world. In an ecosemiotic view, *human language becomes just one among many other semiotic systems in nature that contribute to making the world significant.*

Yet another argument in support of the view that humans are semiotically rooted in nature comes from zoosemiotics, which comprises studies of communication between humans and animals (Sebeok 1990). As is evident from our relations with pets, from various anthropological studies, as well as from human–animal relations in zoos, we are very skilled in establishing relations and communication with other species. Every act of communication, however, presumes shared understanding of, or overlap in, vocabularies, codes, and communication media, so there need to be some levels or modalities in the human semiotic system that make interaction with other species possible. Domestic animals such as dogs and horses are skilled in reading the human gaze, hand gestures, and other nonverbal signals that have been initially part of our communication interactions with other humans (Hare and Tomasello 2005; Joly-Mascheroni et al. 2008; Proops and McComb 2010). The chemical traces that we spread in our body odors during stress, anxiety, or happiness are readable for dogs and emotional states can be mimicked between humans and pets (D'Aniello et al. 2018; Palagi et al. 2015). In research institutions where apes interact with humans, both have been shown to change their communication and use more vocalizations accessible to partner species (Lestel 2002). Thomas A. Sebeok (1991) has called such semiotic modalities by which we participate in communication with other species *zoosemiotic modeling.* These nonverbal aspects of human communication are, however, not separate from language, they inform language and also enter the language system.

A central claim of this Element is that semiotic systems in culture – language, literary works, figurative art, myths, customs – are not closed into themselves, but include semiotic connections with the environment. In other words, there exist semiotic modalities that pass the representation–object divide. In the following pages let us examine a few examples of such semiotic structures as well as some theoretical models to describe these. A general heuristic tool to depart from could be Charles S. Peirce's simple distinction between iconic, indexical, and symbolic signs.[6] This triad describes the relationship between two constituents of the Peircean sign model: the sign (or the representamen) and the object (whereas the third constituent – interpretant – is covered by Peirce's other sign trichotomies). In icons, signs and objects are brought together by similarity. In other words, in icons the sign would bring in mind a similar feeling as the object would, and the sign relation is established because of that resemblance. In indexes, there exists some sort of causal or physical connection between the sign and the object. What the mind tries to establish in the case of an index is an association that would correspond to the underlying processes or patterns of the world. Both icons and indexes may thus establish direct connections between the representations and objects. From an ecosemiotic viewpoint, icons could be said to map the diversity of the things that are there in the ecosystem, while indexes would map the patterns and linkages between these things.

Another classic semiotic typology that can help us articulate different connections between cultural semiotic systems and the environmental processes is Charles Morris' (1971) distinction between the syntactic, semantic, and pragmatic dimensions of semiosis, or in simpler words: between form, meaning, and use of a sign. Whether we focus on natural language, some cultural artefact, or a literary work, these three aspects are probably present and discernable. For instance, on the syntactic level an example of iconicity would be onomatopoeia as the words that gain their meaning because of the resemblance of the vocal pattern to the sounds related to things, beings, or processes that they signify. "Cuckoo" as a name for the bird that emits the sound similar to its name would be a simple example. And although there is a discussion in semiotic and linguistic literature whether the name "cuckoo" is fully onomatopoetic and how it can be that the same bird is called "käki" in Finnish and "Kuckuck" in German, the fact is, that the bird enthusiasts in different countries use their vocal cords to emit the sound similar to the name of the bird to summon the bird successfully to the location. So, whatever the exact phonetic characteristics of the name, in the pragmatic dimension of usage a linkage with the semiotic activities of nonhuman species in an ecosystem is established.

---

[6] What is proposed here, is one possible interpretation and usage of Peirce's semiotic taxonomy among others. Peircean symbols were discussed separately in Section 2.1.

On a more complex level, in the genre of the nature essay the iconicity quite often appears as a mimetic relationship between narrative and some environmental pattern or process. The mimetic capacity of literature in general is a much debated and criticized topic, but nature essays are still often organized according to the track that the author has passed across a specific terrain, according to the advancement of the seasonal changes, or according to a life cycle of the specific animal individual. For instance, in the Estonian tradition, Johannes Piiper (1882–1973), professor of zoology and a renowned nature essayist, organized his writings (Piiper 1935; 1968) as exact observations or travelogues to specific places, including nuanced multisensory depictions equipped with dates and so precise that more than half a century later the footprints of the author can still be easily followed. Thus, the iconic sign relations can bond the structure of narrative and that of the environmental process. If one feels that talking about similarity is theoretically too simplifying in such a case due to the differences in codes, we can apply more complex types of icons such as *diagrams* which Peirce (1931–56: CP 2.277) used to rationalize the correspondence between mathematical graphs and the processes that they represent.

A simple indexical connection between the semiotic system and the environment could be established through deixis, pointing or gesturing. In natural language, pronouns and adverbs such as "this," "she," "there," "now," have a deictic function, by establishing an indexical connection with the context or situation where the language act takes place. In human nonverbal communication, proxemics, hand gestures and grimaces often act as indexical signs. In other animals, indexes are regularly used in the form of odor signs, territorial signs, tracks, and traces (cf. Section. 1.1). As nonhuman animals have more limited capacities for semanticity or referentiality – that is, using signs to denote objects that are distant spatially or temporarily – indexes are very common in animal communication. Indexical signs are often used to demarcate the location or presence of the animal sender, its movement, activities, resources, or other whereabouts. Excrements of a pine marten upon a stone or a tree trunk are an indexical sign, denoting the presence of the animal in the environment. So is the bees' "dance language" in which the circular movement on a honeycomb is used to codify the direction of and distance to the food source. There may also be reason to talk about indexicality in the environment itself, due to the fact that there are overarching regularities in the environmental structures that are interpreted and reacted upon by various species in similar ways and this establishes preferable patterns of interpretation or *ecological codes* (examples of which are interspecies alarm calls of passerine birds or the yellow–black warning coloration in Hymenoptera, Maran 2017a: 129–32). Such environmental indexicality appears to destabilize the boundaries between indexical and symbolic signs in human language as well as between human and other animal sign systems. This peculiarity becomes most obvious in seasonal changes like the arrival of spring:

> In the temperate climate zone, the number of cues, such as the melting of the snow, the arrival of migratory bird species, and the emergence of early flowers, flies, ants and bumblebees can all be representamens referring to the beginning of the spring. At the same time, the question as to what is exactly the object of these representamens, what they refer to, is not so easy to answer. What is this "spring", how to interpret it? Should we limit our understanding with some conventional definition of the word, as: "The season after winter and before summer, in which vegetation begins to appear, in the northern hemisphere from March to May and in the southern hemisphere from September to November"? . . . Or should we include in our understanding of "spring" also the abovementioned perceptual signs of the seasonal change? If so, then there is a reason to distinguish between an astronomical (the period from the vernal equinox to the summer solstice) and a phenologic spring (based on the arrival and life activities of seasonal species etc.), which, depending on the year, can be apart by several weeks. An expression like "the spring is late" would make sense only in cases where these different layers of interpretation are juxtaposed. Furthermore, inasmuch as it is related with the appearance of the early blossoms, the spring emergence of insects and amphibians and the arrival of migratory birds does not depend on just human convention but is related to the interpretations made by other living organisms. When is the right time to return to nesting grounds? When is the water warm enough for spawning? As the human interpretation of the spring at least partly depends on the interpretations done by other living organisms, seasonal change also transforms from being a cultural convention into a natural or ecological convention and is hence a compound environmental sign. (Maran 2017: 365)

As the examples of *compound environmental signs* demonstrate, indexicality can be rooted in environmental processes themselves and in such cases cultural and natural components of semiosis become very difficult to distinguish. Indexicality provides a possibility for human culture to become reconnected with the semiotic fabric of the ecosystem.

In literature, proper names, toponyms, species names as well as descriptions of ecosystems, geographies and weather conditions, factual events and observations obtain a referential function through indexes that connect text with the environment. In the twenty-first century, literary semiotics has paid a lot of attention to the functioning of literary works in their communicative and discursive settings (Sell 2000; Veivo et al. 2009; Johnasen 2002). A scholar central to this tradition, Jørgen Dines Johansen (2002) has proposed a broad perspective to literature by considering: (1) its communicative role between authors and readers; (2) its formal structure and poetics; (3) its subjective and expressional qualities; and (4) referential capacity to express the world outside literature. Especially in regard to the latter dimension, indexical properties of literature come into spotlight. Johansen and Svend Erik Larsen (2002: 84–5) have distinguished three types of indexes as those that involve reference (designation) to the real world, to the discourse itself, and to an ideal possible world. They claim that indexes establish both the connection between the text and the communicative situation as well as make it possible to distinguish between the discursive universe and the real world. The Peircean scholar Vincent Colapietro (2009: 112–13, 118) further specifies that indexes in literary texts have an essential role in "calling us to the things of this world" and "pointing things out" for us as the fictional world "draws massively upon the familiarity of our everyday world." Especially in nature writing, referential linkages to ecological conditions, ecosystems, living conditions, and habits of different animal and plant species are important, as they make it possible to educate the readers, raising their awareness of and competence in ecological processes. Indexicality and environmental literacy are closely related. Here, indexicality becomes a source of information shared and instructions given as to what there is in nature, what to notice, and how to relate to the particular environment, how to take care of it. Because of indexes, literature helps us to direct our attention to subtle things in nature that would otherwise escape our notice altogether, as other species would remain hidden from us due to the differences in scale, communication media, or living habits.

From an ecosemiotic perspective, we can pay more detailed attention to the role of the environment in literary creation and in literary works. The semiotic potential of the environment as well as semiotic and communicative activities of other species indeed inspire literary creation, act as targets of indexical reference of literature, or as sources of interpretation going on in parallel with that of literary texts. Sometimes we can also witness how literary creation shapes the cultural meanings and landscape use of specific locations as has happened with Walden Pond in Massachusetts, USA, or with Vilsandi Islets in Western Estonia (Maran and Tüür 2017). In such cases, the text, the environment, and the agencies of the author and readers enter into complex interplays that shape the literary experience as well as functioning of the literature in the real world. Indexical references appear to have various directions and modes in nature writing. This was the original idea that I have tried to convey under the concept of "nature–text" (Maran 2007). More recently, I have, however, become critical of the possibility of delineating the four constituents of this model – text, nature, author, reader – in any clean and organized manner. Rather, nature–text appears to enfold as a field of interactions or polylogues between different semiotic actors and subjectivities (including these in the environment and text). Sometimes a written text really becomes immersed in the environment: intra- and extradiegetic appearances of the author, inclusion of natural codes and conventions, and folk narratives that the text depends on make the text a heterogenic meshwork of various meanings, voices, and narratives. For analyzing literary work in such conditions,

> an elaborate model of the relations between the text and the environment is needed as a tool for analysis. . . . The formal characteristics of nature writing – the literary and narrative strategies employed in the text – are often organised and shaped according to the particular environmental relationship it represents. Thus, the nature-text model asks what kind of literary devices are there to convey what kind of human-environment relation (message) in the context of what kind of environment. (Maran and Tüür 2017: 290)

As I hope to have shown in these pages, the self-enclosure of the human symbolic culture is not an inevitable, nor even a very realistic situation. There are many possibilities on the nonverbal level, in pragmatic actions of sign, in iconic and indexical semiosis, for connections to emerge between culture and ecosystems. Culture can be reconnected with the ecosystem and there are semiotic tools suitable for this.

2.3 The Necessity of Dialogue

Yes, but why bother? Why should we be concerned about the role of nature in literature, why should writers, artists, and literary scholars pay attention to spiders, birds, trees, and moss? There are indeed serious environmental problems in our time such as global warming, decline of biodiversity, and accumulation of waste, but solutions to these will most probably be provided not by humanities but by technological sciences and engineering. So why should humanities scholars be concerned with environmental issues, why does it matter to what degree culture consists of iconic and indexical sign or how culture relates to the environmental semiosis and communicative activities of other species?

A possible answer to these questions is actually rather simple. The relationship between nature and culture does not have an effect only on ecosystems, but on culture as well. *Having rich and diverse relations with the natural environment is essential for the well-being and proper development of human culture.* This thesis derives from a number of sources, but one of them is Juri Lotman's (2005: 5–6) understanding of communication. Lotman stated that communication takes place and is valuable not because of the overlapping and shared parts between the participants but because of what is different between them. What is overlapping between the participants is what is already known and trivial to them and the main function of this part is just to establish communicative contact. "It appears that the value of dialogue is linked not to the intersecting part, but to the transfer of information between nonintersecting parts. This places us face-to-face with an insoluble contradiction: we are interested in communication in the very sphere which complicates communication and, in actual fact, renders it impossible" (Lotman 2005: 6). Such type of dialogue may take place in autocommunication as between different phases of the ego, between the center and the periphery of culture, or on a temporary scale between different cultural epochs. In Lotman's view, and this is in striking contrast with other well-known communication models (e.g. by Shannon and Weaver or Jakobson), communication does not lead to unity and similarity between the participants, but is, on the contrary, a source of creativity and novelty in culture. This idea brings along a radical shift in thinking about the diversity – the *other*, the *different* is not valuable for its own sake, but because without being in contact with the other the *self* itself would degenerate.

To project this idea of Lotman's onto the ecological domain, nature is essentially important for the culture due to nature's otherness, strangeness, hiddenness, and partial inconceivability. Nature is a place of discovery, but not only as concerns itself, but more importantly as regards culture. Italian semioticians Susan Petrilli and Augusto Ponzio (2005: 35ff; Petrilli 2003: 95) proposed a similar idea in their semioethics project. Reflecting on the works of Charles S. Peirce, Mikhail Bakhtin, Emmanuel Levinas, and Victoria Welby, they claimed that dialogic relations with the other are an indispensable pre-requisite for normal semiosis and should thus be considered a basic human right. Depending on the context and the situation, the other can be a human partner, a pet, a good book, a foreign language, or natural environment – whatever challenges perception and thinking, whatever allows us to express human behaviors such as attending, compassion, and caring.

Where does this need for dialogue originate and why is it so fundamental for the flourishing of semiotic and living systems? I think that most generally, the need for the other derives from our belonging to the world, or, to put it in a more technical language, from coupling and feedback between a unit and the system to which the unit belongs. This is the relationship that enables rejuvenation, adjustment, and adaptation of the self in relation to the never-ending changes taking place in ecosystems. The dialogic encounters are just the ways in which the world in its multitude is exposed to us. Ecophenomenologist David Abram has related the necessity to be in contact with nonhuman others with our evolutionary past, claiming that an environment rich in sights and sounds was an original context in which our senses evolved:

Our bodies have formed themselves in delicate reciprocity with the manifold textures, sounds, and shapes of an animate earth – our eyes have evolved in the subtle interactions with other eyes, as our ears are attuned by their very structure to the howling of wolves and honking of geese. To shut ourselves off from these other voices, to continue by our lifestyles to condemn these other sensibilities to the oblivion of extinction, is to rob our own senses of their integrity, and to rob our minds of their coherence. We are human only in contact, and conviviality, with what is not human. (Abram 1997: 22)

British biosemiotician and ecocritic Wendy Wheeler has opened the future-oriented aspect of the very same relation in the beautiful metaphor of "expecting the Earth":

all organisms human and non-human *expect the Earth*. We are made in it, and remade in each generation in that expectant relation to things. For us in our material presence, we expect things that have not yet come to be, but which wait to enfold us. Thereby we arrive to become opened up to further, a lifetime's relations. *That* is what life is. (Wheeler 2016: 2012)

So, the dialogic relations with others – be it material environment or its living habitants – have enabled us to reach our current cognitive and sensory capacities and at the same time these encounters also open up novel perspectives on the future. The common denominator here appears to be the role of the context, the very fact that semiotic and living systems cannot develop in an empty space. Every semiotic and living entity relies in its growth and dynamics on contacts with things that it itself is not. This thought is in accordance with Gregory Bateson's (1972: 185, 244) idea that learning always takes part in a particular communicative context and as it is eventually about this context, the two cannot be effectively separated from each another. Biosemiotician Jesper Hoffmeyer (2007), who was influenced by Bateson's thought, introduced the concept of *semiotic scaffolding* to explain the role of context in living systems. He claimed that from a single cell to highly social species, organisms use entities of their surrounding environment as building blocks in their development toward new skills and cognitive capacities. For instance, young ibexes defy steeps and cliffs as counter-structures for learning how to move in their rocky habitat; a human child can use his/her fingers as aids in learning counting. When the necessary skills are acquired, the scaffolds lose their role as learning aids but become a part of the further cognitive structures, e.g. the male ibex can strategically use the mountain terrain to increase success in mating fights or children can use fingers as a means to gesture numbers to one another. In short, all living and semiotics systems need some sort of counter-structures, constraints, or boundary conditions for normal functioning. Relations with these "others" are essentially dialogic as they work through expressing, making use of, responding, and accommodating.

Dialogic relations with the environment as the "other" depend upon nonsymbolic signs. It is designation, pointing to the other, inclusion of onomatopoetic utterances, empathy arising from similarities and associations through which communication is opened to the other. Symbols, on the other hand, are by definition arbitrary and conventional. This means that *symbols function effectively only for people who share the communication code and who are part of a given convention*. Symbols operate through homogeneity. In order to conduct a dialogue with the other, however, some cracks need to be opened in the symbolic system, some inconsistences need to emerge through which more spontaneous sign activities can unfold and the other agencies can enter semiosis.

The position of human culture is more complex here, as culture itself is normally heterogenic and contains possibilities for dialogue and autocommunication within itself between different parts, subjects, texts, and phases. Nevertheless, lack of contact with other species and the material world may undermine the chances for cultural dialogue and development. Semiotician Riin Magnus reminds us that in twentieth-century philosophy (e.g. in the works of Martin Buber, Hans Jonas) and especially in relation to the *end of nature* debate, there is a constant concern with the loneliness and solitude of the human species (Magnus 2012). Despite technological progress and reaching the most remote corners of the world, humans have become solitary, as other species have ceased to address us, to ascribe meanings to us, whereas their dominant reactions toward us have become avoidance and fear. Magnus points out that the condition of the modern human, which in religious terms has been interpreted as being abandoned by God, may in fact be "man's deviation from the ecologically meaningful existence" (Magnus 2012: 162). And is the very progress of modern culture, its endeavor to fill all the silence with sounds, our houses with various technological items, our attention to overly ornate discourses and aggressive images, not at least partly a reaction to this unbearable emptiness that rises from lack of "others" that could give meaning and significance to life?

Culture that has lost dialogic relations with its environment is in danger of collapsing under its own weight. This is the tragedy of accumulating positive feedback. If a person or a culture becomes surrounded by nothing other than its own reflections, little sanity will remain. There are possibilities for the culture to heal from the situation, but this cannot occur straightforwardly. A magic trick is needed. The problem at stake here is that it is not easy to evoke the other as a *true other* in a way that would not be just a mere reflection or amplification of one's own image. This shift cannot be achieved in the frame of a given cultural symbolic hegemony that is only able to repeat its habits, but there needs to be an agency capable of destabilizing and interrupting the existing conventional codes and symbolic systems. This was the role of the forest deity Pan in Greek mythology and fools and clowns in medieval courts. In cultural theory the same functionality has been described by Michel Serres in his interpretation of the parasite and by Gregory Bateson as *epistemology of the sacred*. In particular, Gregory Bateson's last book *Angels Fear*, composed together with his daughter Mary Catherine (Bateson, Bateson 1988), was concerned with mechanisms in individual consciousness and in culture that regulate and restore the balance between the sign activity and its conditions or context. Bateson's understanding was based on the recognition that there is an inevitable epistemological gap between the mental process and the conditions of that very mental process (for instance, between thinking and the physiological processes in the body that enable thinking). "Sacred" was a key word for Bateson to denote the phenomena by which the integration is restored across the epistemological gap, but not through communication that would only extend the sphere of knowing at the cost of things known. Some other means and modalities like taboo, ritual or art are needed for integration. "The sacred (whatever that means) is surely related (somehow) to the beautiful (whatever that means)" (Bateson 1979: 235–6). The sacred is essential for the sustainability of culture as it makes possible the corrective shifts between human thoughts and their context in the world. Michel Serres' parasite tells us another and perhaps crueler part of the same story. This is the tale of worms, rats, satyrs, jokers, cheaters, and other unpleasant characters in culture and nature. Serres' parasite is a disruption in the symbolic order, the third that blends into and feeds upon the system by producing noise, uncertainty, and confusion. "The parasite dis-accords, makes noise" (Serres 2007: 133), "Noise destroys and horrifies. But order and flat repetition are in the vicinity of death. Noise nourishes a new order" (Serres 2007: 127). "The bit of noise, the small random element, transforms one system or order into another. To reduce this otherness to contradiction is to reduce everything into violence and war" (Serres 2007: 21). Parasites in nature or in human society may be annoying, but at the same time the disturbance that they create is indispensable for renewal and thus for long-term sustainability of cultural systems.

At times of global environmental change we would need to restore the dialogicity of culture more than ever. Unstable climate, movement of species, and rise of oceans with their various aftereffects challenge human cultures to be more adaptive and transformative. Making sense of the meanings of the environmental change is, however, almost impossible in a state of being detached from the environment and its various inhabitants who all bear their own experiences of the changing world. The same applies to human social groups, who tend to lock themselves into closed and contradicting discourses without any chance of cultural dialogue and development. This is why philosopher of science Michel Callon and his colleagues (2009) have proposed that for handling an uncertain environment with unknown problems creating "hybrid communities" of many different competences could be the best strategy. A group of people with many different professions, skills, and experiences would have a large space for the differences and hence possibilities of reaching, through dialogue, a solution suitable for the given situation. In a similar way I have highlighted the importance of multispecies communities in which local human communities also include other species. The idea of multispecies communities is based on broadening human value judgments in a way that the essential role of other species in creating and preserving livable environment for an entire multispecies community would be acknowledged. Multispecies communities would also rest on the understanding of the indispensable need for the other. The adaptation and adjustment of other species may be the necessary source of inspiration for human culture to cope with the changing world.

Helping to understand and restore the connection between culture and nature as a dialogic situation may be a positive contribution from ecosemiotics. Such connections could lead the way to a greater biocultural diversity and ecocultural resilience as a capacity of local nature–cultures to withstand social and environmental turbulences (Pilgrim and Pretty 2013: 11). What is required is, in fact, a systemic change of cultural conventions or codes, an approach that would enable us to open symbol systems to other sign modalities as well. Semiotics has conceptual tools to scrutinize the sign relations between culture and nature, to understand how they work, why they have ceased to function, and what can be done to restore the dialogue. The modeling system theory developed by the Tartu-Moscow School of Cultural Semiotics is a suitable starting point for such analysis, as I will demonstrate in Section 3. In principle, attention can be paid to several topics: using semiotic models for shifting and destabilizing the border between representations and objects; creating possibilities for nonhuman semiotic agencies to take part in cultural semiosis; presenting animal *Umwelten* in cultural texts; and changing grounds of modeling by finding analogies from nature. The latter option will be exemplified in Section 3.3 by a thought experiment of modeling text or culture as a forest.

3 Healing by Modeling

3.1 An Ecosemiotic Reading of Juri Lotman's Semiotics

There are pieces of literature that have the capacity to make people reconsider the ways in which they live. There are also texts that may make us change the ways in which we interact with the nonhuman world. At the birth of the ecocritical movement in the 1970s, William Rueckert (1978) observed that poets are like green plants and can convert warmth of the sun into textual energies that somehow make their readers change. Here, some poems that have inspired you may come to mind. Let me quote a poem by the Estonian poet Jaan Kaplinski (1985):

> *Our Shadows*
> *are very long*
> *when we return at night from haying*
> *but we ourselves are small*
>
> *The camomile clasps its hands together*
> *as if in prayer*
> *A woman with a sickle creeps up the hill*
> *as she did a thousand years ago*
> *Beyond the courtyard*
> *the heath*
> *beyond the heath forest*
>
> *Heather heather-colored*
> *whither dost thou fly little bee*
> *that heaven*
> *is so vast and void*
> *once we will return*
> *once we will all return.*

I have long felt that Rueckert's essay, despite its metaphoricity, or perhaps precisely because of it, nailed something very essential about culture–nature relations. His idea that imagination has something to do with organic growth, that poetry belongs to the same living cycle with plants and animals, is deeply ecological. It may just be that semiotics provides us with a better language for conveying such thinking – understanding in what ways the interactions between the literature and ecosystem are played out and how they function. As argued in the earlier sections, for an ecosemiotic view the material environment has a semiotic potential. Various animal species (including humans with their culture) are taken as participating in meaning-making, but they do so on different levels. Human culture is predominantly symbolic, which makes it semiautonomous in its relations to natural environments and ecosystems, and also makes it possible for culture to change and modify nature. However, as argued earlier, human culture also consists of simpler sign types that enable connection between humans and the environment. Previously we have described this dynamics of different signs in culture–nature relations as follows:

> Human semiotic involvement in the environment is hybrid by nature. On one hand, everything that humans do involves (biogeo)chemical and energetic aspects, element cycles, and energy flows. In this sense, cultural processes are

always situated within the chemical and energetic processes of an ecosystem, culture is physically part of the ecosystem. On the other hand, in terms of semiotic processes, the situation of culture is twofold. First, cultural semiotic processes form a part of the semiotic processes of an ecosystem as a local web of all semiotic processes. Second, cultural models can be the models of this system itself. In this sense, culture as a modelling system builds up a meta-level in relation to the ecosystem. (Maran and Kull 2014: 45)

Thus, models and modeling stand at the heart of culture–nature relations. The concept of modeling refers back to Tartu-Moscow School of Cultural Semiotics and the works of its leading figure, Juri Lotman. In the following pages, I will provide a short introduction to Lotman's intellectual world and discuss the applicability of his concepts to ecosemiotics and environmental humanities. I believe that this could provide us with a general framework for understanding the dynamics of signs between literature and ecosystems.

Juri Lotman (1922–93) was a renowned Russian literary scholar and semiotician. He graduated from Leningrad State University in Russian language and literature, and, after difficulties in obtaining a position in Russia due to his Jewish heritage, he reached the University of Tartu in Estonia in 1950. He held several positions at the Department of Russian Literature at the University of Tartu up to the 1990s (Andrews 2003: 6–7). In the early 1960s Lotman started a collaboration with semiotics scholars from Moscow (Vladimir Toporov, Vyacheslav Ivanov, Boris Uspenskij, and others), issuing collective publications on semiotics and modeling systems, and conducting a series of seminars held at Kääriku, Estonia. This intellectual development became known as the Tartu-Moscow School of Cultural Semiotics.

As Lotman was a linguistics and literature scholar by education, topics of the environment were not central for him. At the same time, Lotman's style of thinking was rich in combining, synthesizing, and elaborating various influences, and these influences also included biological sciences. Several commentators (Kull 2015; Patoine and Hope 2015; Andrews 2003; Mandelker 1994) have interpreted Lotman's thinking as a gradual shift from structuralism to poststructuralism and organicism, in the course of which physiological and biological underpinnings of culture were taken into account.[7] Verging between structuralism and poststructuralism, Lotman created a unique understanding of culture that relates topics such as cultural autocommunication as a memory mechanism, relations between different entities in culture through modeling and

---

[7] For instance, Lotman's ideas of asymmetry between different parts of the semiosphere and, in relation to this, incompatibility as a situation of partial translatability with accompanying need for several languages in culture was metaphorically derived from the different functioning of the left and right hemisphere of the human brain.

translation, novelties rising in culture's inner and outer boundaries, dynamics between center and periphery, and alternation between stable and unstable periods of cultural development. Many of these concepts are potentially relevant for ecosemiotics and can be elaborated in the contexts of environmental humanities.

Lotman was not uninterested in nature. At a young age, he developed a fascination with biology, especially entomology, and was even planning to specialize in biology at university (Patoine and Hope 2015). His son Aleksei Lotman was later active at the Zoology Department at the University of Tartu, working on the psychology of apes, which, together with the emerging connections with the circles of theoretical biology in Tartu and Leningrad (St. Petersburg), created a thread of discussion in human–animal relations for Juri Lotman in the 1980s. Approximately at the same time Juri Lotman developed his probably best-known concept of the *semiosphere* as a semiotic space of cultural texts, processes, and interactions (for a more thoroughgoing review of relations between Lotman's cultural semiotics and biological sciences, see e.g. Kull 1999; 2015). According to Lotman the essential characteristics of the semiosphere are the existence of multiple languages, the presence of boundaries, inherent irregularities, and asymmetries between different parts of the semiosphere in translation, and other cultural processes (Lotman 2005). The idea of the semiosphere was loosely based on the concept of the biosphere introduced by the Ukranian geologist Vladimir Vernadski (1997) in the early twentieth century (although the Lotman specialist Amy Mandelker [1994] also emphasizes Mikhail Bahktin's influence on Lotman's organicist thinking). There were other similar ideas in the air in the mid twentieth century; for example Teilhard de Chardin's noosphere and Bakhtin's logosphere, but only the approaches of Vernadski and Lotman appear to be intrinsically systematic and ecological. Vernadski's idea of the biosphere was based on understanding the enormous role of the living processes shaping the earth, the specificity of the growth of living organisms compared to inorganic matter, and the exchange of matter and energy between the living and the inorganic worlds. Similarly, Lotman's concept of the semiosphere emphasizes the role of semiotically organized space before any single constituents of the sphere. "The semiosphere is the result and the condition for the development of culture" (Lotman 1990: 125). Texts cannot exist outside of the semiosphere as there can be no organisms living outside of the biosphere. Kaie Kotov and Kalevi Kull have explained how the concept of the semiosphere expresses the predominance of semiotic processes: "semiosphere is a sphere of semiosis and an experience thereof; and as such, it is a prerequisite for any single act of communication to be interpreted as one" (Kotov and Kull 2011: 180). The position that semiosis precedes any

formal structures and codes provides an essential role for cultural dynamics –
dialogues and translation between different texts, dynamics between inner
speech and texts, andrelations between internal and external space are essential
for the normal functioning of culture. "A semiosphere enters into dialogic
relations with other semiospheres, as well as nurturing dialogue within itself
in the interactions between its interior elements and their correlative functions"
(Mandelker 1994: 389). Lotman's concept of the semiosphere can thus be
interpreted as a move away from structuralist thinking and semiotic totalitar-
ianism and toward establishing a more ecological understanding of culture.

Independently from Lotman, the concept of the semiosphere was also used by
Jesper Hoffmeyer (1996) to denote the sum of all semiotic and communicative
processes on the planet. According to Hoffmeyer: "the semiosphere is a sphere
just like the atmosphere, the hydrosphere, and the biosphere. It penetrates to
every corner of these other spheres, incorporating all forms of communication:
sounds, smells, movements, colors, shapes, electrical fields, thermal radiation,
waves of all kinds, chemical signals, touching, and so on. In short, signs of life"
(Hoffmeyer 1996: vii). Another interpretation of the semiosphere that connects
culture and nature was proposed by American medievalist and ecosemiotician
Alfred K. Siewers who used the term *ecosemiosphere*. According to him, "an
ecosemiosphere literally means an ecological bubble of meaning (borrowing
the term 'semiosphere' from semiotics). It involves not a 'reenchantment' of
nature, but recognition of nature as a meld of physical and cultural communication, which can be considered spiritual as well as material" (Siewers 2014: 4),
and the term also "extends earlier definitions of specific symbolic cultures as
semiospheres, or meaningful environments, into physical environments"
(Siewers 2011: 41). In developing an ecosemiotic interpretation of the concept
of the semiosphere, Kalevi Kull's (2004: 184) elaboration of the semiosphere in
the form of the *ecosphere* as a *space of diversity* seems essential. The sugges-
tions made by these authors indicate that the diversity of the semiosphere
probably goes beyond humans and incorporates both the semiotic activities of
other species as well as semiotic potentials of inanimate nature.

In the following, let us pick three ideas from the rich inheritance of Juri
Lotman's cultural semiotics that, when interconnected, provide a good framework for ecosemiotics and environmental humanities: (1) autocommunicative
capacities of culture; (2) semipermeable boundaries between cultural and extracultural spaces; and (3) understanding of space as a semiotically active entity.

1. *Autocommunicative capacities of culture.* For Lotman, an important property of culture is its ability to relate to itself by obtaining different roles and
   using different languages in forming autocommunicative loops, to provide

"food" for its own semiotic receptors and inputs. In autocommunication, some shift in meanings needs to take place that is achieved by inclusion and combination of more than one language or code. Autocommunication provides culture with an ability to look at itself from aside, to put itself in the position of an object that results in self-reflection, self-description, and translating one-self into a meta-layer and creation of new languages of description (Lotman 1997). Autocommunication is a mechanism enabling a number of essential properties of culture such as rejuvenation, identity, and memory. Culture is constantly engaged in various autocommunicative and self-modeling processes, examples of which are literary and fine arts, translation, cultural criticism, humanities, and philosophy (Torop 2008: 393). For instance, every critical reflection of a literary work shapes the understanding of the writing in question, but also becomes itself a part of culture, by developing the culture's self-understanding. Understanding autocommunication as a central mechanism of culture also paves the way for reinterpreting the role of the humanities and cultural criticism, as these become processes of self-perception and self-modeling of the culture. In the context of ecosemiotics and environmental humanities, this would mean that analyzing nature-writing and other culture–nature engagements will be made with the aim of providing culture with a better understanding of different ways and capacities of how the culture can relate with ecosystems.

2. *Semipermeable boundaries between cultural and extracultural space.* Cultural boundaries are related to the subjectivity of culture and its functioning in autocommunication. According to Lotman, for culture to be semiotically active, a certain enclosure, definiteness and self-sufficiency is needed (Lotman 1997). Culture projects its boundaries outward to limit the space where its own semiotic rules and codes are valid. However, these boundaries of culture are not absolute but relative, more like reflections necessary for the functioning of the culture. For Lotman, the idea of the cultural boundary was based on a biological analogy. Lotman builds his understanding on the analogies with the living cell: culture adopts the outside influences by selecting and translating these into its own semiotic system similar to a cell that accepts chemical elements for these to become processes of its biochemical functioning (Lotman 2005: 210). Another biological analogy that Lotman uses to imagine boundaries of culture is sensory receptors, which transfer external stimuli into the language of our nervous system (Lotman 2005: 209). The boundaries of culture are selective semi-transparent or semi-permeable membranes that act as translation mechanisms between the culture and its surrounding space by selectively admitting and blocking various influences. Boundaries both separate and

unite and therefore the outer border of the semiosphere becomes a region of increased semiotic activity (Lotman 1990: 136).

This also means that the existence of the space external to the semiosphere is both essentially important for the functioning of the culture as well as accessible under certain conditions (a diversity of languages, rapid cultural change). The space outside of the culture may have semiotic potentiality for a number of reasons: for example, it can be organized by other cultures or semiospheres; it can contain fragments of the activities and material artefacts of earlier cultural eras that are forgotten and thus cast out of the culture (Maran 2014b). From an ecosemiotic perspective, also extracultural space itself may have a semiotic potential due to the structures and patterns of the physical environment and communication with other species. Let us observe, in a few longer quotations, how Lotman describes the relations between cultural and extracultural space:

> the relationships between the translatable and the untranslatable are so complex that possibilities for a breakthrough into the space beyond the limits are created. This function is also fulfilled by moments of explosion, which can create a kind of window in the semiotic layer. Thus, the world of semiosis is not fatally locked in on itself: it forms a complex structure, which always "plays" with the space external to it, first drawing it into itself, then throwing into it those elements of its own which have already been used and which have lost their semiotic activity. (Lotman 2009: 24)
>
> The border of semiotic space is the most important functional and structural position, giving substance to its semiotic mechanism. The border is a bilingual mechanism, translating external communications into the internal language of the semiosphere and vice versa. Thus, only with the help of the boundary is the semiosphere able to establish contact with nonsemiotic and extrasemiotic spaces. As soon as we move into the realm of semantics, we have to appeal to an extrasemiotic reality. (Lotman 2005: 210)
>
> ... it is necessary to emphasise the fact that the boundary, which separated the closed world of semiosis from extra-semiotic reality, is permeable. It is constantly transgressed via intrusions from the extra-semiotic sphere, which, when bursting in, introduce a new dynamic, transforming the bounded space and simultaneously transforming themselves according to its laws. At the same time, semiotic space constantly ejects all the layers of culture from itself. The latter form layers of deposits beyond the limits of culture and await their time to re-enter the closed space by which time they are so "forgotten" as to be conceived of as new. Such exchanges with the extra-semiotic sphere create an inexhaustible reservoir of dynamic reserves. (Lotman 2009: 115)

To conclude, in Lotman's view, culture can come in contact with extracultural space, and these contacts can be sources of creativity and dynamics in culture. At the same time, the semiotic transmissions with the extracultural space need a translation mechanism – certain structures or models in culture that make the interactions possible. To communicate with the external space, culture needs to have its "nerves" or "channel proteins." If we attempt to convey this idea to ecosemiotics and environmental humanities, then, it appears that in order to pay attention to and take care of the environment, culture needs to include effective cultural forms and models that could make this translation possible. We could ask what exactly are the properties that make works of art (novels, movies, paintings) effective in translating environmental semiosis into culture (see Section 3.2 on this). Studying the functioning of the works of art that act as such models can be a task for ecosemiotics.

3. *Space as a semiotically active entity.* Lotman's understanding of the extra-cultural space seems to be ambivalent. There are a number of occasions in Lotman's work when the space outside of culture is treated as semiotically void, while only cultural languages are seen as able to make outer space meaningful for culture (Lotman 1990: 124, 134). In some texts, Lotman claims that it is culture itself that disorganizes the external space to create an asymmetry with the cultural organization: chaos, barbarians, waste are thus projected outside of the limits of culture (Lotman 1990: 142). Such ideas are probably reflections of earlier modernist thinking in Lotman's works. Culture can also project its imagined spatial organization onto the material environment, in which case the tangible space may become an expression of culture's idealized order (on that and other examples of spatial thinking in Lotman, see Remm 2015). However, in his later writings Lotman also attributed semiotic activity to the physical space by describing the latter as another primary modeling system – a concept of the Tartu-Moscow School of Cultural Semiotics that was mostly used to denote natural language (cf. Section 3.2). Especially, Lotman ascribed the status of a modeling system to structured space – by the latter he primarily meant phenomena that transcend the homomorphic structure of space and that create asymmetric structures (e.g. shadows, reflections on water, echoes) (Lotman 1992). Understanding space as a primary modeling system is related to Lotman's understanding of art that, differently from language, is based on nondiscrete continuous sign systems. The whole discussion is important for understanding if and under what conditions in Lotmanian semiotics nature itself can become semiotically active and a dialogue partner for culture.

There are some secondary interpretations of Lotman's work that open interesting perspectives on this topic. Landscape semiotician Kati Lindström has linked the concepts of landscape, space, and autocommunication. She takes up Lotman's observation that a monk walking and contemplating in a stone garden can be interpreted as an example of autocommunication (Lotman 1990: 25), and analyzes different properties, spatial and rhythmic markers, of Japanese landscapes to describe the role that these can have in personal autocommunication (Lindström 2011: 39; Lindström 2010). Autocommunication in Lotman's sense is a process in which, by involvement of a second language, code, sign system, or because of a shift in context, some sort of alteration is created and a situation of dialogue between different phases of the first person emerges (Lotman 1990: 21). Autocommunication has mnemonic and creative functions. Lindström (2010) observes that

> ephemera, human everyday rhythms, cosmological and seasonal rhythms, perceptual stimuli – can be considered as a secondary code leading to autocommunication in the person who contemplates the landscape. Looking at the landscape – which also implies rhythmical movements of the eyes – one uses it as a code to reconstitute oneself. A person who has confronted a landscape does not leave it as the same person. (Lindström 2010: 371)

The environment has its patterns, rhythms, and inner structures and due to these it can be a source of a second code or language for culture and restructure the communicative process. In this process, the otherness of the environment is essentially important, as it is this distance or tension between culture and nature that triggers the autocommunicative process. These encounters between culture and nature are no locations of suppression and violence but, on the contrary, sources of novelty and creation.

What seems essentially important for environmental humanities is Lotman's view of culture as dynamical and regulatory in its relations with the extracultural space. Lotman does not, at least in his later works, treat culture as all-encompassing, yet neither does he try to remove the difference between culture and nature, nor does he describe the border between nature and culture as impenetrable. Rather, culture keeps its subjectivity, autonomy, and dynamics, but does this in relations with the outer space that allow culture to change and regulate itself in relation to the surroundings. These relations are essential for the dynamism and rejuvenation of culture. The boundaries of culture are not passive, but reminiscent of activity centers where changes of the culture can take place and novelties can emerge. Lotman's thinking thus provides us with a framework in which to work with cultural texts as models for altering the core structures of culture that are related to valuing environment as well as the relations between culture and the environment.

3.2. Literature as a Model of the Human–Nature Relationship

A central concept of the Tartu-Moscow School of Cultural Semiotics is that of modeling systems. The term that originated from cybernetics and linguistics was employed to understand the functioning of literature, art, and other cultural phenomena (Zaliznjak et al. 1978). Juri Lotman has explained that a modeling system "is a structure of elements and rules of their combination, existing in a state of fixed analogy to the whole sphere of the object of perception, cognition, or organization" (Lotman 2011: 250). An exemplary case of a modeling system is natural language, but there are also secondary modeling systems, systems of systems – art, religion, myth – that make use of the means of language to model reality. According to Lotman, a specific feature of these secondary modeling phenomena is that they do not rely on a single language but create models by combining the languages of the genre, cultural epoch, social group, idiosyncratic languages of the author, etc. Using various languages, a model is created as "an analogue of an object of perception that substitutes it in the process of perception" (Lotman 2011: 250). This analogue, however, is not based on simple similarity or mimesis but built onto crossroads between the represented features of the perceived object and the capacities of the given sign systems. Lotman's cultural text as a model balances the properties of the symbolic sign system with indexical reference and iconic resemblance (cf. Nöth 2018). Instead of being simple representing, modeling can thus be seen as a more complex process of translation or recoding. Literary semiotician Jørgen Dines Johansen (2002: 164–5) explains:

> According to Yuri Lotman (1967), literature, as a model, is an iconic representation, or an analogue, of the object it represents. The individual model belongs to a modelling system, and literature is a so-called secondary modelling system, that is, a system built upon language as the primary modelling system. A modelling system consists of an inventory of elements and their combination rules and it holds an analogical relation to its object. The literary work of art is, at the same time, both a representation of the object by means of the system's elements and relations and its analogue.

Differently from technical modeling in mathematics and other sciences, artistic modeling is not fixed and determinate but creative, and includes a degree of freedom and playfulness. The artistic model is thus a complex and multilayered entity that provides a rich space for possible interpretations (Lotman 2011: 265–6). Its elements are often polysemantic and ambiguous, entering into complex interrelations with one another. For instance, a literary work can simultaneously contain multiple perspectives or alternate ways to understand the activities of the characters and is thus open to many possible interpretations. This makes artistic modeling also a very efficient tool for communicating human experience. It may even be said that modeling is *hologrammic* in the sense that it conveys rich and multivariate information in a very constrained form.

Despite their complex structure and allowing for multiple interpretations, artistic models retain a certain iconic relationship with their objects and can act as substitutes for the object in the processes of thinking, feeling, and communication. This analogy-based or iconic relationship is not, however, all-encompassing – the model represents its objects in certain aspects or qualities, while the specifics of this relation itself have a lot of semiotic significance and meaning. "The model represents a homomorphic representation, i.e. not identical to the original. It means the representation in the sense of the Latin 'pars pro toto': 'the part instead of the whole'" (Tondl 2000: 83). It is exactly this type of relation between the original and the model in which the cultural tradition, the discipline, and the author's worldview become involved and make a difference. Consequently, in addition to different languages and codes involved in modeling, we also have reason to distinguish the *ground* of modeling as a question of which feature or image has been employed as the basis of comparison in creating the model. The concept of the ground has been more often used in Peircean semiotics to denote those properties of the two things entering into the sign function by means of which these get connected (Sonesson 2010: 28). Grounds can also be more complex, like relations by the *tertium comparationis* in metaphors or even more-fuzzy images of thought in the case of fictional and utopian literary works. Examples of grounds used to model the natural environment and its inhabitants could be analogies with or metaphoric relations to dominant cultural topics (such as anthropomorphism, sociomorphism, linguamorphism, technomorphism, cf. Komarek 2009: 108ff). For instance, techomorphic or mechanomorphic modeling takes a "machine as an exemplary being and interprets the world through analogy to it" (Komarek 2009: 109). Understanding how different languages and types of signs are employed in the modeling process and how the resemblance is built by using grounds of comparison equips us with better access to the semiotic relations between literature and the environment (see also Section 3.3).

There has been a noticeable shift in the twenty-first century in understanding the unity and wholeness of the literary text. This is an important point as it relates directly to the question of how the object can be represented in text by means of modeling. In early literary semiotics of the 1960s and 1970s the text was often seen as a distinct entity (Eco 1979: 7). Also Lotman repeatedly stressed the borders or the closed nature of the literary work as its identifying criteria (Lotman 1978; Lotman and Piatigorsky 1978). In the twenty-first century, however, developments in media technologies have shifted attention from a distinct literary work to intersemiotic and transmedial links between different cultural entities. The possibilities and necessities to make adaptations between various media (literature to film, opera to comics, film to video games, etc.) have destabilized the identity of the single literary work (cf. Ojamaa and Torop 2015). Allusions, cross-references, loans, covers, copying, mixing, and blending are anything but rare in contemporary culture; rather, they emerge as common forms of cultural creation. Often the manifestations of original texts become so scattered over different media, genres, and texts that it makes sense to talk of literary clouds, imaginative worlds or universes. Loss of unity of the single text in literary semiotics, however, may help us also reach a more complete understanding of the modeling relations between text and the environment in the ecosemiotic frame. The analogy-based modeling relations between the text and environment remain, but they become contextualized by other types of semiotic relations. These additional relations emerge because of the semiotic potentiality of the environment and activity of its inhabitants to become engaged in meaning making. For instance,

> text and the environment can be in a complementary relationship so that the reader's experience of the text and of the environment become actualised simultaneously in the reading process, and mutually support each other. In such a case, not all the meaning relations potentially present in the environment need to be represented in the text, yet the author presumes that his/her readers are familiar with the common characteristics and properties of the environment. In case of a complementarity relation, interpretative loops emerge between the text and the environment; the text is interpreted with reference to the environmental experience and the environment is interpreted on the basis of textual knowledge. (Maran and Tüür 2017: 290)

Aside from complementary relations between the text and patterns of the environment, there are a number of animals in nature who make themselves noticeable by vocal calls, specific appearance, and action. The question here arises in what ways the communicative expressions of other species are conveyed in literary works, how and by what discursive means the voice and subjectivity is lent to nonhuman animals. As an example of such vivid animal expression, we can recall the gaze of the dying wolf in Aldo Leopold's essay "Thinking Like a Mountain" and its role in inspiring the author to develop land ethics: "We reached the old wolf in time to watch a fierce green fire dying in her eyes. I realized then, and have known ever since, that there was something new to me in those eyes something known only to her and to the mountain. I was young then, and full of trigger-itch; I thought that because fewer wolves meant more deer, that no wolves would mean hunters' paradise. But after seeing the green fire die, I sensed that neither the wolf nor the mountain agreed with such a view" (Leopold 1968: 130). Drawing on a number of examples of birdsong, calls, and other sounds represented in nature writing, Kadri Tüür (2009; 2016) has suggested that such cases could be considered *biotranslation*, translation between species. The core of the idea of biotranslation is that there is something in the *Umwelt* of one species that enters the *Umwelt* of another species being mediated by the accessible sign systems (Kull and Torop 2003). Tüür's suggestion was that the concept of biotranslation could also be used to describe connections between animal vocalizations in the wild and their representations in literary works.

We can see that the semiotic relations between the text and the environment are diverse. Within its limits the text acts as a model of the environmental relations, but the two also interact in a complementary and dialogic fashion. The semiotic processes taking place in the environment become the counterpart (cf. Section 3.1 on space as a semiotically active entity) needed to make sense of what the written text is about. Such complementarity can be seen as a form of Lotmanian autocommunication, that is, due to different sign systems and languages active in the text and in the environment, the two, when interpreted together, become a nucleus of cultural creativity and novelty.

I have argued earlier that each work of nature writing can essentially be considered a model of the human–nature relationship, with respect to both the actual and the ideal state of that relationship (Maran 2014a). That is, each written text about nature can tell us something about the ways in which humans interact with nature, either with an emphasis on the existing relationship (essays departing from the author's personal experience), relationships to be avoided (works of environmental writing with a critical emphasis), or relations that are not present but should be (eco-utopias, environmental fiction). To understand how literary works represent human–nature relationships, we should focus on how different types of signs participate in this. Looking at a literary work in an ecosemiotic frame transforms the role of signs as the broader context of environmental semiosis is taken into account. Icons and indexes become means by which the text is connected with the ecosystem (through biotranslation, designation, cf. Section 2.2), whereas the symbolic layer conveys the identity of the text and carries values concerning the human–nature relationship. This shift of perspective also means that I should moderate my earlier criticism of the hegemony of cultural symbols (discussed in Section 2.1). Symbols in discourses, sign systems or texts are not malevolent *per se*, but only if they become over-imposed so that they suppress iconic and indexical signs and, by doing so, break the relation with life and dialogic exchange in the ecosystem. Is not the symbolic dominance, in fact, the very mechanism present at the center of every autocratic or extremist ideology that strives to establish a closed symbolic space and to expand it by silencing everyone and everything around them? In an ordinary organically developing discourse or culture, however, symbols have their role and function next to icons and indexes. What should be paid attention to, is ways in which these different types of signs can be combined to create patterns that allow us to say something significant about the world.

In previous studies, I have suggested distinguishing between zoosemiotic, linguistic, and artistic modeling layers when analyzing nature writing or other texts related to the environment (Maran 2014a). This distinction was based on the typology of primary and secondary modeling systems in the Tartu-Moscow School of Cultural Semiotics and is roughly parallel to Peirce's categories of firstness, secondness, and thirdness. There are also further possibilities to elaborate modeling systems theory for literary analysis, as proposed for instance by Thomas A. Sebeok and Marcel Danesi (2000).[8] Broadly speaking, zoosemiotic modeling relies on our physiological capacities, bodily sensations, and multisensory perception. The concept derives from the works of Sebeok, according to whom humans use their *Umwelt* structures, sensory organs, and nervous system, as well as the corresponding capacities of action and behavior, to model the surrounding world (Sebeok 1991). In nature writing, zoosemiotic modeling creates a phenomenological presence for the reader, an experience of the "here and now" that allows the reader to associate him-/herself with the nature experience of the author. Zoosemiotic modeling is iconic in the sense that it evokes feelings that are similar to the original nature experience. Linguistic modeling has a referential function; it conveys information and factual data about the represented environment, ecosystems, and species, and it can point to practical knowledge and utilitarian value of the environment, its resources, and inhabitants. Linguistic modeling is indexical in the sense that it depends on the actual world of nature and on the readers' knowledge of it. Artistic modeling creates the poetic space of the author in a literary work. On the level of artistic modeling the author uses poetic, stylistic, and narrative means to convey his/her abstract ideas, appreciations and value judgments. In the case of nature writing, artistic modeling is often used to communicate the author's ideals about culture–nature relations. Artistic modeling is symbolic in the sense that it is independent from any specific nature experience and through it we can recognize the particular literary work's individuality and identity.

I have used the proposed modeling theory in analyzing a particular text of nature writing – the essay "The Thistle" written by the well-known Estonian nature writer Fred Jüssi (1986). The detailed analysis has been published in the journal *Green Letters* (Maran 2014a), but it could be worth discussing here the relations between different modeling types to show their roles and interconnectedness. All modeling types were present in the essay that I discussed. For

---

[8] Thomas A. Sebeok and Marcel Danesi (2000) distinguish between the following modeling types: singularized modeling (sign-based), composite modeling (text-based), cohesive modeling (code-based), and connective (metaphoric) modeling.

instance, zoosemiotic modeling was located at the beginning and end of the text, where it framed the essay and provided perceptual access to the reader. Artistic modeling was intermittently employed for the author's philosophical observations about anthropophilic species, the natural way of life and human destiny. It appears that the balance between different modeling layers may be crucial in communicating healthy human–environment relations. For instance, "without the other modelling levels, linguistic modelling runs the risk of turning into a 'manual' of the environment and thus eventually triggering the impact that humans exert on the environment as a result of classifying nature and then subjecting it to exploitation in accordance with the classification" (Maran 2014a: 308). In a similar way, the over-dominance of artistic modeling threatens to turn the environment in a text into a mere decoration, a stylistic ornament, thereby shutting off the possibility of interference from nonhuman voices and agencies. Even if applying this method on other texts and discourses is still waiting for its time, attending to how different sign types and modeling layers work in interaction in a broader ecological context may be a key to developing a healthy ecological discourse. Iconic and indexical signs are needed for maintaining dialogic relations between cultural texts and ecosystems, while the symbolic component ensures the continuation of ecological views in culture.

3.3 Semiotic Models for Reconnecting Culture and the Ecosystem: The Example of the Model of the Forest

We could open up human culture to environmental semiosis and communicative activities of other species by knowingly altering the grounds of modeling used to make sense of the nonhuman world. Modeling in culture often takes more familiar things as a basis for understanding things that are more distant to us. The German cultural semiotician Walter A. Koch (1986: 54) has called such analogy-based modeling the *autoanalytic* approach and considered it to be the most primordial cognitive scheme in humans. An exemplary case of this strategy is anthropomorphism – describing behavior of other animals in comparing them to similar activities of our species and valuing other species based on the properties that they share with humans. For instance, late twentieth-century cognitive ethology, comparative psychology, and zoosemiotics (e.g. Griffin 1976; Sebeok 1981) debated as to what degree communication systems of nonhuman animals resemble human language and if any other species would in principle be capable of learning human language. This interest resulted in a number of ape language projects such as the ones with the chimpanzee Washoe (by Beatrix T. Gardner and R. Allen Gardner) and the bonobo Kanzi (by Sue Savage-Rumbaugh) (see Westling 2016). The underlying issue in this debate was not, however, a genuine interest in the skills and capacities of apes, dolphins, or parrots, but more the ethical question of whether species should be paid attention to and valued in a way that follows the same principles that are applied to humans. Language that was considered to be a defining property of humans obtained the role of a measuring device, a ground for comparison in these discussions.

Another widespread and problematic type of modeling uses binary opposi-tions or other simple schemas of contrast as a basis for meaning-making. Here, simplified oppositions between human and animal, city and wilderness, texts and reality, native and alien species establish discontinuities in thinking.[9] Simplified grounds for modeling tend to influence nature through human action and severely limit the possibilities for human culture to become integrated in ecosystems (Kull 1998; Maran and Kull 2014; Augustyn 2013). Thinking in binary models also often forces us to take sides, ignore the intermediate, and promote the preferred option at the expense of the other. At the same time, semiotic modeling allows us to create playfully new bases of comparisons that are more complex and integrative. One possibility would be to take some phenomena from nature and analogically transpose them so that they become a model that can then be used as a new basis for modeling. Such an approach could be, in principle, applied in both artistic and literary creation, as well as on the meta-level as a criterion for theoretical analysis. In the following pages I will consider the forest as a possible ground for semiotic modeling and ask what kind of possibilities and properties such modeling image could bring forth.[10] My intention is not to treat the forest as a semiotic system – which I think it is – but rather to ask: If we use the forest as a semiotic model to analyze some other object, what new perspectives would such an approach open? In order to answer this, I will first reflect on the forest as a temperate ecosystem from an ecological perspective.

In ecological vocabulary the main autotrophs and primary biomass producers in a forest are trees, which also provide ecological niches for many other organisms. A specific component of the forest ecosystem is the decay cycle involving various decomposers (insects, worms, fungi) and a bulk of fallen

---

[9] A close theoretical approach to semiotic modeling is that of cognitive framing deriving from cognitive linguistics (mostly based on works of George Lakoff) and discourse analysis. Gregory Bateson (1972), from whom this approach largely proceeds, connects framing with the theory of logical types. Cognitive framing has more to do with the contextual rules of interpreting messages in discourses, whereas semiotic modeling pays attention to the constitution and referential structure of the texts themselves. For applications of framing in environmental topics, see e.g. Weik von Mossner (2018).

[10] A more elaborate version of this analysis is available in Maran (2020a). Forest has been used as a heuristic metaphor also by Eduardo Kohn (2013) and Umberto Eco (1994).

leaves and woody debris that provides nutrients to insects and other inverte-
brates, rodents, and many other creatures living on the forest floor (Chapin et al.
2011: 183ff). A large amount of the biomass (up to 60 percent, Lukac and
Godbold 2011: 26) in forests lies below the ground. For an ecological view,
a characteristic of the forest is the presence of several interconnected structural
layers. These can be mapped spatially, temporally, or structurally, as different
layers of the vertical structure in vegetation, different stages of succession, or
different levels of the ecological pyramid. Natural forests are characterized by
the presence of trees of different ages and different species: there are always
young trees, overgrown trees, fallen trees, as well as the under-bush and herb
layer with seedlings. Such layering provides structural or spatial diversity in the
sense that due to differences in microgeography, the development of trees and
the effects of wind and fire, forests are usually patterned or patchy. It also
provides conditions for many different ecological niches as well as space for
a complex network of interspecies relations.

As is the case with many other ecosystems, forests are autopoietic entities, in
the sense that they are capable of renewing themselves and restoring themselves
after natural or human-induced disturbances (Messier et al. 2013). Many forest
ecosystems are resilient to quite significant changes (e.g. clearings caused by
storms or forestry management), and some are even dependent on the physical
effect of elemental forces (e.g. forest fires, floods) in their rejuvenation (Peh
et al. 2015). As an ecosystem, the forest significantly modifies its own conditions; for instance, the temperature and humidity in forests can be different
compared to the surrounding open environments. Such dynamics are not based
on any fixed or hierarchical control system, but result from the abundance of
living matter in forests as well as the local regulatory feedback cycles between
various species. Taking the forest as a ground for semiotic modeling could bring
forth and highlight properties of the analyzed objects that more conventional
semiotic models would overlook. There are five key properties of the forest as
a semiotic model that I would like to highlight:

1. *Distributed communication codes.* Forests are inhabited by a great number
   of species with different physiologies and *Umwelten*. These species also use
   · different communicative means – sign systems and communication codes –
   yet at the same time they are able to communicate with one another and give
   positive or negative feedback to one another. What makes such communication possible is the partially shared communicational conventions that can be
   called *ecological codes* (see Section 2.2., Maran 2012; Kull 2010).
   Ecological codes are not general rules but distributed conventions: every
   participant uses a partial variation of a code. The same principle of

ecological codes can be broadened to the forest as a semiotic model. When you move in the forest, the environment that surrounds you changes. With every step, new views and perspectives will open up, and earlier views, experiences, and options will close. You will move from the partial variations of the semiotic code to new variations. There is no single background system, no unifying language, but the semiotic rules or codes themselves are changing. Using the forest as a semiotic model would thus emphasize that every locus of the object has its own semiotic character or quality. Situatedness in the forest is the case by default, and the neutral position of the observer is a special condition.

2. *Tolerance of meaning.* The forest is rich in ecological relations between different species. In these relations, two or more species – which often have very different life habits and life necessities – interact. It would follow that meaning-relations are mutual – meanings are not just perceived and interpreted but also attributed and, on behalf of the communication partner, accepted and carried. These two sides of semiotic relations develop simultaneously, wielding a reciprocal influence. When you walk in a forest, you may notice different birds, recognize their species, and attribute meanings to them. At the same time, other living organisms perceive your presence and attribute meanings to you based on their *Umwelt* structures. It is not enough to know the sign systems and codes used in the semiotic system; the more crucial question is to what degree semiotic subjects of a given system endow a human with meanings. What is specific about the forest as a semiotic model is this general architecture of relations. Every species is in relation to the manifold other inhabitants of the forest, and therefore the acceptance of, or submission to, meanings tends to outweigh the outbound semiotic activity of the subject. This process, which Jakob von Uexküll (1982: 59–62) calls the *tolerance of meanings*, is the dominant form of the semiotic activity in the forest. The tolerance of meaning appears to be a central notion in understanding human involvement in any complex semiotic system.

3. *Local heterogeneity and creativity.* Deriving from the two previous characteristics, in the semiotic model of the forest the basic unit of analysis should be a focal point where semiotic activities of different participants and local conditions meet and are actualized. The focal points in the forest are distributed unevenly, and they have different qualitative properties. They are active, creative, and poetic, and the meanings that grow in them cannot be deduced from the surrounding conditions nor from the inner properties of the organisms involved. It is not an exaggeration to say that the forest grows through these focal points or nodes or, in other words, that the local configurations in the forest-like semiotic model change and recreate the

reality of the forest as a broader system. The node as a basic unit of analysis also indicates that describing the forest in its entirety is hardly possible. On the one hand, this is due to the local creative dynamics and, on the other hand, to the unboundedness of the forest. In its entirety, the forest is more complex than any possible description of the forest; the number of its different possible relations is immeasurably vaster.

4. *Strong ontological presence.* In forests, features, meanings, and qualities are not just accidental phenomena but strong ontological properties of the living beings and the environment. Meanings and qualities do not derive from the subjects' interpretations, but meaning potentials are embodied in the bodies of animals and in the physical structures of the ground. The forest as an environment makes certain interpretations possible, while it constrains others. To give a practical example, if you take the wrong turn in a forest, you will be in danger of getting lost. An animal that is not attentive enough to its surroundings is in danger of being caught and preyed upon. The forest gives quick and effective feedback to the perceptions, interpretations, and actions of a semiotic subject. The strong ontology is related to the historical dynamics of the forest. The strong ontology allows us to interpret the history of the forest – to the professional eye, the forest is an open book about the growth of trees, about past clearings and human actions, forest fires, and wind damage. Such interpretation would not be possible without a certain reality of the forms of the landscape. For the forest as a semiotic model, this means that its semiotic structures are motivated: content and form are related to each other, and arbitrariness is rare, occasional, and constrained.

5. *Surplus of semiotic material.* The forest in an ecological sense is characterized by many decay chains, the existence of abundant debris and dead organic matter. In the forest as a semiotic model, semiotic processes are flourishing, overwhelming, and there is a surplus of semiotic material. Various signs and texts are used simultaneously, either in support of one another or in contradicting or comparative ways. This overflow of signs is a reason (besides diverse communication codes) why the forest as a semiotic model cannot be formal or arbitrary – forms and contents are related loosely and do not constitute a unified semiotic system. The forest as a semiotic model also contains a lot of semiotic material that is not actively used or interpreted at the moment but that is in a passive stage or forgotten, or that remains in various stages of degradation and decay. Unused and forgotten semiotic sources have a huge potential to be reused, reorganized, filled with new meanings, and put into use in new relations, in new nodes of the forest as a system. Emphasizing the relevance of the decay change would also mean that reuse, adaptation, and remodeling are common strategies in such

a semiotic system: emerging signs coopt earlier semiotic structures, which can be remainders of previous semiotic material or have a foreign origin (cf. semiotic cooption, Kleisner 2010; Maran and Kleisner 2010). For applying forest-based semiotic modeling to other semiotic phenomena (texts, cultures, and languages), the creative potential of the partial, incomplete, and decaying semiotic material needs to be taken into account (recently, Donna Haraway [2016] has argued for the "compost" and "compost-ist" as suitable terms to describe human creative effort in the Anthropocene to overcome boundaries of culture, species, and kin). This would also mean blurring the binaries: borders of the forest, life and dead matter, culture and nature.

Let us now sum up the basic properties of the forest model. I have claimed that in the forest as a semiotic system, meanings and codes are shared partially in variations; being in the forest means tolerating meanings and becoming an object of meaning attribution; the basic unit of analysis in the forest is a focal point or node where semiotic activities and local conditions meet; characters, meanings, and qualities have strong ontology and history; and there is a surplus of semiotic material beyond the currently active semiotic processes. To provide an even shorter description, the forest model would describe an object of analysis as heterogeneous, with its own ontology, locally regulated and accidental, but at the same time well integrated. So what would happen if we tried to use the forest as a model to read a book, to interpret a culture, or to make sense of another human being? Using forest-based modeling could provide us with new reading experiences or research strategies. Such an approach would focus on particulars and their different engagements, it would pay attention to idiosyncratic languages and semiotic fragments. It would involve a human subject who, by being engaged in local variations and by being willing to tolerate meanings, could again become a part of the ecological whole.

Afterword

There is no snow. In my more than forty years of life experience, the winter of 2019/20 was the first one in Estonia without snow cover. The white ground has made the long dark Nordic winters more bearable, but not this year. I know that seals in the Baltic Sea are in trouble because they need an ice sheet on which to give birth to their cubs. Sleepless and hungry brown bears are wandering somewhere in forest clearings not far from here. Nature is changing and this touches culture as well. A lot of beautiful poetry has been written in Estonian about winter landscapes and the impressions these leave on the human psyche. There is also a rich vocabulary in the Estonian language for different types of snowfall, snow, and ice: "räitsakas" (large, slowly falling snowflake), "lobjakas" (hard, wet and windy snowfall), "kirmetis" (whitish barely visible film in the ground or water), "rüsijää" (ice crushed to the shore), and so on. All of this with vanishing referents now. Timothy Morton (2013) has proposed the concept of *hyperobjects* to denote entities – nuclear waste, plastics, climate change – that, due to their endurance and reach, exceed the limits of any human reference frame or discourse. My worries go in the opposite direction. In global environmental change there are no steady objects, no background systems that would remain stable to act as reference points for culture. There are no reliable scaffolds for any living system to hold on to, no context for meaning-making. All clocks are lying. All metrics bent. In such conditions the survival of human culture will increasingly more depend on its abilities of adaptation, its dialogue with the nonhuman world, local adjustments, and inventiveness.

I hope to have shown with this Element that causes for this Anthropocenic condition are largely semiotic – based on our striving toward symbolic hegemony and preference of closed semiotic systems. Still, I have also shown that this ideal has actually never succeeded. There are still plenty of options for simpler iconic and indexical signs in human culture that have the potential to reconnect culture with the ecosystem and to be used to establish dialogues. An openness to dialogues is essential for the healthy dynamics of human culture. Furthermore, living nature itself, the ecosystem, is predomin-antly semiotic by being based on sign regulation in its cach and every joint. There is a readiness for dialogue in the nonhuman world, an interest in making sense of human doings and in attributing meanings to us. In the face of global environmental change, humans and other animals appear to stand on the same page as we all need to find novel ways of living in an environment that is becoming increasingly more strange. In such conditions, we need to learn from one another. The decisive question at this turning point becomes the dialogicity of culture, the willingness to become engaged. Dominique Lestel has written: "Imagination is a collective activity resting largely on the space of possibles revealed to us by the species with which we share our life. [T]oday's collapse of biodiversity is not only a biological catastrophe that will prevent finding new medicines (Boeuf 2007), it is also, and perhaps above all, an existential catastrophe that substantially reduces the extent and complexity of our imagination and consequently of our humanity itself" (Lestel 2013: 311). Thinking with other species and using them as the source of our imagination can directly aid us in finding new and workable strategies for adjusting to the changing environment. In this process literature and art have a central role, as artistic models can reach across the culture–nature border and act as gateways to translate between different semiotic domains. Also Lotman's semiotic modeling can be used here as a creative approach for finding new grounds for meaning-making that would embrace the agency of other species and environments, and build anew the connections with the rest of the ecosystem. Ecosemiotics can contribute to environmental humanities by indicating some mechanisms by which such dialogues can be initiated.

In Tartu, Estonia, February 2, 2020

References

Abram, D. (1997). *The Spell of the Sensuous*. New York: Vintage Books.

Agosta, S. J. and Klemens, J. A. (2008). Ecological fitting by phenotypically flexible genotypes: Implications for species associations, community assembly and evolution. *Ecology Letters*, **11(11)**, 1123–34.

Andrews, E. (2003). *Conversations with Lotman: Cultural Semiotics in Language, Literature, and Cognition*. Toronto: University of Toronto Press.

Augustyn, P. (2013). Man, nature, and semiotic modelling or how to create forests and backyards with language. *Sign Systems Studies*, **41(4)**, 488–503.

Bateson, G. (1972). *Steps to an Ecology of Mind*. San Francisco: Chandler.

Bateson, G. (1979). *Mind and Nature. A Necessary Unity*. Toronto: Bantham Books.

Bateson, G. and Bateson, M. C. (1988). *Angels Fear: Towards an Epistemology of the Sacred*. Cresskill: Hampton Press.

Bleicher, S. S. (2017).The landscape of fear conceptual framework: Definition and review of current applications and misuses. *PeerJ*, 5:e3772: doi.org/ 10.7717/peerj.3772

Bradbury, J. W. and Vehrencamp, S. L. (2011). *Principles of Animal Communication. 2nd ed.* Sunderland: Sinauer.

Bruno, J. F., Stachowicz, J. J. and Bertness, M. D. (2003). Inclusion of facilitation into ecological theory. *Trends in Ecology & Evolution*, **18(3)**, 119–25.

Callon, M., Lascoumes, P. and Barthe, Y. (2009). *Acting in an Uncertain World: An Essay on Technical Democracy*. Cambridge, MA: Massachusetts Institute of Technology Press.

Candland, D. K. (2005). The animal mind and conservation of species: Knowing what animals know. *Current Science*, **89(7)**, 1122–7.

Chapin, F. S., Matson, P. A. and Mooney, H. A. (2011). *Principles of Terrestrial Ecosystem Ecology*. New York: Springer.

Clark, A. (1997). *Being There: Putting Brain, Body and World Together Again*. Cambridge, MA: Massachusetts Institute of Technology Press.

Cobley, P. (2016). *Cultural Implications of Biosemiotics (Biosemiotics vol. 15)*. Dordrecht: Springer.

Colapietro, V. (2009). Pointing things out: Exploring the indexical dimensions of literary texts. In H. Veivo, C. Ljungberg and J. D. Johansen, eds., *Redefining Literary Semiotics*. Newcastle upon Tyne: Cambridge Scholars Publishing, 109–33.

Cowley, S. J. (ed.) (2011). *Distributed Language*. Amsterdam: John Benjamins.

Damásio, A. (1994). *Descartes' Error: Emotion, Reason, and the Human Brain*. Berkley: Putnam Publishing.

D'Aniello, B., Semin, G. R., Alterisio, A., Aria, M. and Scandurra, A. (2018). Interspecies transmission of emotional information via chemosignals: From humans to dogs (Canis lupus familiaris). *Animal Cognition*, **21(1)**, 67–78.

De Santana, C. N., Rozenfeld, A. F., Marquet, P. A. and Duarte, C. M. (2013). Topological properties of polar food webs. *Marine Ecology – Progress Series*, **474**, 15–26.

Eco, U. (1976). *A Theory of Semiotics*. Bloomington: Indiana University Press.

Eco, U. (1979). *The Role of the Reader: Explorations in the Semiotics of Texts*. Bloomington: Indiana University Press.

Eco, U. (1994). *Six Walks in the Fictional Woods*. Cambridge, MA: Harvard University Press.

Emmeche, C., Kull, K. and Stjernfelt, F. (2002). *Reading Hoffmeyer, Rethinking Biology. (Tartu Semiotics Library vol. 3.)* Tartu: Tartu University Press.

Farina, A. (2006). *Ecology, Cognition and Landscape: Linking Natural and Social Systems*. Dordrecht: Springer.

Farina, A. (2008). The landscape as a semiotic interface between organisms and resources. *Biosemiotics*, **1(1)**, 75–83.

Farina, A. (2012). A biosemiotic perspective of the resource criterion: Toward a general theory of resources. *Biosemiotics*, **5(1)**, 17–32.

Farina, A. and Belgrano, A. (2004). The eco-field: A new paradigm for land-scape ecology. *Ecological Restoration*, **19**, 107–10.

Farina, A. and Belgrano, A. (2006). The eco-field hypothesis: Toward a cognitive landscape. *Landscape Ecology*, **21**, 5–17.

Farina, A. and Pieretti, N. (2013). From Umwelt to soundtope: An epistemo-logical essay on cognitive ecology. *Biosemiotics*, **7(1)**, 1–10.

Gibson, J. J. (1979). *The Ecological Approach to Visual Perception*. New Jersey: Lawrence Erlbaum.

Gilbert, S.F. and Epel, D. 2008. *Ecological Developmental Biology: Integrating Epigenetics, Medicine, and Evolution*. Sunderland: Sinauer Associates.

Goodale, E., Beauchamp, G., Magrath, R. D., Nieh, J. C. and Ruxton, G. D. (2010). Interspecific information transfer influences animal community structure. *Trends in Ecology & Evolution*, **25(6)**, 354–61.

Griffin, D. R. (1976). *The Question of Animal Awareness: Evolutionary Continuity of Mental Experience*. New York: Rockefeller University Press.

Gulick, W. (2012). Polanyian biosemiotics and the from-via-to dimensions of meaning. *Tradition and Discovery: The Polanyi Society Periodical*, **39(1)**, 18–33.

Hagen, J. B. (1992). *An Entangled Bank: The Origins of Ecosystem Ecology.* New Brunswick, NJ: Rutgers University Press.

Haraway, D. (2016). *Staying with the Trouble: Making Kin in the Chthulucene.* Durham, NC: Duke University Press.

Hare, B. and Tomasello, M. (2005). Human-like social skills in dogs? *Trends in Cognitive Sciences,* **9(9)**, 439–44.

Hoffmeyer, J. (1996). *Signs of Meaning in the Universe.* Bloomington: Indiana University Press.

Hoffmeyer, J. (2007). Semiotic scaffolding of living systems. In M. Barbieri, ed., *Introduction to Biosemiotics.* Dordrecht: Springer, 149–66.

Hoffmeyer, J. (2008). *Biosemiotics: An Examination into the Signs of Life and the Life of Signs.* Scranton: University of Scranton Press.

Hornborg, A. (1999). Money and the semiotics of ecosystem dissolution. *Journal of Material Culture,* **4(2)**, 143–62.

Hornborg, A. (2001). Vital signs: An ecosemiotic perspective on the human ecology of Amazonia. *Sign Systems Studies,* **29(1)**, 121–52.

Janzen, D. H. (1985). On ecological fitting. *Oikos,* **45(3)**, 308–10.

Johansen, J. D. (2002). *Literary Discourse. A Semiotic-Pragmatic Approach to Literature.* Toronto: University of Toronto Press.

Johansen, J. D. and Larsen, S. E. (2002). *Signs in Use. An Introduction to Semiotics.* London: Routledge.

Joly-Mascheroni, R. M., Senju, A. and Shepherd, A. J. (2008). Dogs catch human yawns. *Biology Letters,* **4(5)**: doi.org/10.1098/rsbl.2008.0333

Jordan, L. A. and Ryan, M. J. (2015). The sensory ecology of adaptive landscapes. *Biological Letters,* **11**, 20141054: dx.doi.org/10.1098/rsbl.2014.1054

Jørgensen, S. E. (1992). *Integration of Ecosystem Theories. A Pattern.* Dordrecht: Springer SBM.

Jørgensen, S. E. and Müller, F. (2000). Ecosystems as complex systems. In S. E. Jørgensen and F. Müller, eds., *Handbook of Ecosystem Theories and Management.* Boca Raton: Lewis Publishers, 5–20.

Jüssi, Fred (1986). Ohakas [Thistle]. In Fred Jüssi, *Jäälõhkuja [Icebreaker].* Tallinn: Valgus, 35–6.

Kaplinski, J. (1985). Three poems. *The Paris Review,* **96, 99**: www.theparisreview .org/poetry/2900/three-poems-jaan-kaplinski Accessed 15.01.2020.

Kleisner, K. (2010). Re-semblance and re-evolution: Paramorphism and semiotic co-option may explain the re-evolution of similar phenotypes. *Sign Systems Studies,* **38(1/4):** 378–92.

Koch, W. A. (1986). *Evolutionary Cultural Semiotics: Essays on the Foundation and Institutionalization of Integrated Cultural Studies.* Bochum: Brockmeyer.

Kohn, E. (2013). *How Forests Think: Toward an Anthropology Beyond the Human.* Berkeley: University of California Press.

Komárek, S. (2009). *Nature and Culture. The World of Phenomena and the World of Interpretation.* München: Lincom Europa.

Kotov, K. and Kull, K. (2011). Semiosphere is the relational biosphere. In C. Emmeche and K. Kull, eds., *Towards a Semiotic Biology: Life is the Action of Signs.* London: Imperial College Press, 179–94.

Kull, K. (1998). Semiotic ecology: Different natures in the semiosphere. *Sign Systems Studies,* **26,** 344–71.

Kull, K. (1999). Towards biosemiotics with Juri Lotman. *Semiotica,* **127(1–4),** 115–31.

Kull, K. (2004). Semiosphere and a dual ecology: Paradoxes of communication. *Sign Systems Studies,* **33(1),** 175–89.

Kull, K. (2010). Ecosystems are made of semiosic bonds: Consortia, umwelten, biophony and ecological codes. *Biosemiotics,* **3(3),** 347–57.

Kull, K. (2015). A semiotic theory of life: Lotman's principles of the universe of the mind, *Green Letters,* **19(3),** 255–66.

Kull, K. and Torop, P. (2003). Biotranslation: Translation between umwelten. In S. Petrilli, ed., *Translation Translation.* Amsterdam: Rodopi, 313–28.

Laigle, I., Aubin, I., Digel, C., Brose, U., Boulangeat, I. and Gravel, D. (2018). Species traits as drivers of food web structure. *Oikos,* **127,** 316–26.

Lakoff, G. and Johnson, M. (1980). *Metaphors We Live By.* Chicago: Chicago University Press.

Lakoff, G. and Johnson, M. (1999). *Philosophy in the Flesh: The Embodied Mind and Its Challenge to Western Philosophy.* New York: Basic Books.

Latour, B. (1993). *We Have Never Been Modern.* Cambridge, MA: Harvard University Press.

Leopold, A. (1968). *A Sand County Almanac, and Sketches Here and There.* Oxford: Oxford University Press, 129–33.

Lestel, D. (2002). The biosemiotics and phylogenesis of culture. *Social Science Information,* **41(1),** 35–68.

Lestel, D. (2013). The withering of shared life through the loss of biodiversity. *Social Science Information,* **52(2),** 307–25.

Lévêque, C. (2003). *Ecology: From Ecosystem to Biosphere.* Boca Raton: CRC Press.

Lindström, K. (2010). Autocommunication and perceptual markers in landscape: Japanese examples. *Biosemiotics,* **3(3),** 359–373.

Lindström, K. (2011). *Delineating Landscape Semiotics: Towards the Semiotic Study of Landscape Processes. (Dissertationes semioticae Universitatis Tartuensis, 15).* Tartu: University of Tartu Press.

Lotman J. (1978). Problems in the typology of texts. In. D. P. Lucid, ed., *Soviet Semiotics: An Anthology*. Baltimore & London: Johns Hopkins University Press, 119–24.

Lotman, J. (1990). *Universe of the Mind. A Semiotic Theory of Culture.* Bloomington: Indiana University Press.

Lotman, J. (1992) = Лотман, Юрий Михайлович. "Текст и полиглотизм культуры". (Text and Cultural Polyglotism) – *Лотман, Ю. М. Избранные статьи в трех томах. т. I. Статьи по семиотике и топологии культуры. Таллин: Александра*, 142–7.

Lotman J. (1997). Culture as a subject and an object in itself. *Trames*, **1**(1), 7–16.

Lotman, J. (2005). On the semiosphere. *Sign Systems Studies*, **33**(1), 215–39.

Lotman, J. (2009). *Culture and Explosion. (Semiotics, Communication and Cognition 1)*. Berlin: Mouton de Gruyter.

Lotman, J. (2011). The place of art among other modelling systems. *Sign Systems Studies*, **39**(2/4), 249–70.

Lotman, J. and Piatigorsky, A. M. (1978). Text and function. In. D. P. Lucid, ed., *Soviet Semiotics: An Anthology*. Baltimore & London: Johns Hopkins University Press, 233–44.

Lukac, M. and Godbold, D. L. (2011). *Soil Ecology in Northern Forests. A Belowground View of a Changing World*. Cambridge: Cambridge University Press.

Lupien, S. J., Maheu, F., Tu, M., Fiocco, A. and Schramek, T. E. (2007). The effects of stress and stress hormones on human cognition: Implications for the field of brain and cognition. *Brain and Cognition*, **65**(3), 209–37.

Magnus, R. (2012). How did man become unaddressed? In T. Maran, K. Lindström, R. Magnus and M. Tønnessen, eds., *Semiotics in the Wild: Essays in Honour of Kalevi Kull on the Occasion of his 60th Birthday*. Tartu: University of Tartu Press, 157–63.

Malavasi, R., Kull, K. and Farina, A. (2014).The acoustic codes: How animal sign processes create sound-topes and consortia via conflict avoidance. *Biosemiotics* **7**(1), 89–95.

Mandelker, A. (1994). Semiotizing the Sphere: Organicist Theory in Lotman, Bakhtin, and Vernadsky. *Publications of the Modern Language Association*, **109**(3), 385–96.

Maran, T. (2007). Towards an integrated methodology of ecosemiotics: The concept of nature-text. *Sign Systems Studies*, **35**(1/2), 269–94.

Maran, T. (2010). Why was Thomas A. Sebeok not a cognitive ethologist? From "animal mind" to "semiotic self". *Biosemiotics*, **3**(3), 315–29.

Maran, T. (2012). Are ecological codes archetypal structures? In T. Maran, K. Lindström, R. Magnus and M. Tønnessen, eds., *Semiotics in the Wild:*

Essays in Honour of Kalevi Kull on the Occasion of his 60th Birthday. Tartu: University of Tartu Press, 147–56.

Maran, T. (2014a). Biosemiotic criticism: Modelling the environment in literature. *Green Letters: Studies in Ecocriticism*, **18**(3), 297–311.

Maran, T. (2014b). Semiotization of matter: A hybrid zone between biosemiotics and material ecocriticism. In S. Iovino, and S. Oppermann, eds., *Material Ecocriticism*. Bloomington: Indiana University Press, 141–54.

Maran, T. (2017a). *Mimicry and Meaning: Structure and Semiotics of Biological Mimicry. (Biosemiotics vol. 16)*. Cham: Springer.

Maran, T. (2017b). On the diversity of environmental signs: A typological approach. *Biosemiotics*, **10**(3), 355–68.

Maran, T. (2020a). Deep ecosemiotics: Forest as a semiotic model. *Recherches sémiotiques / Semiotic Inquiry (RS/SI). Special issue on Biosemiotics. ed. J. Bates. Forthcoming.*

Maran, T. (2020b). Ecological repertoire analysis: A method of interaction-based semiotic study for multispecies environments. *Biosemiotics*, 13(1), 63–75.

Maran, T. and Kleisner, K. (2010). Towards an evolutionary biosemiotics: Semiotic selection and semiotic co-option. *Biosemiotics*, **3**(2), 189–200.

Maran, T. and Kull, K. (2014). Ecosemiotics: main principles and current developments. *Geografiska Annaler: Series B, Human Geography*, **96**(1), 41–50.

Maran, T. and Tüür, K. (2017). From birds and trees to texts: An ecosemiotic look at Estonian nature writing. In J. Parham and L. Westling, eds., *A Global History of Literature and the Environment*. Cambridge: Cambridge University Press, 286–300.

Messier, C., Puettmann, K. J. and Coates, K. D., eds. (2013). *Managing Forests as Complex Adaptive Systems: Building Resilience to the Challenge of Global Change*. London: Routledge.

Morris, C. (1971). Foundations of the theory of signs. In Charles *Morris, Writings on the General Theory of Signs*. The Hague: Mouton, 17–71.

Morton, T. (2013). *Hyperobjects: Philosophy and Ecology after the End of the World*. Minneapolis: University of Minnesota Press.

Nielsen, S. E. and Herrera, A. Y. (2017). Sex steroids, learning and memory. In D. W. Pfaff and M. Joëls, eds., *Hormones, Brain and Behavior*, 3rd ed. Amsterdam: Academic Press, 399–422.

Nielsen, S. N. (2007). Towards an ecosystem semiotics: Some basic aspects for a new research programme. *Ecological Complexity*, **4**(3), 93–101.

Nielsen, S. N. (2016). Second order cybernetics and semiotics in ecological systems – Where complexity really begins. *Ecological Modelling*, **319**, 119–29.

Noble E. E., Hsu T. M. and Kanoski, S. E. (2017). Gut to brain dysbiosis: mechanisms linking western diet consumption, the microbiome, and cognitive impairment. *Frontiers in Behavioral Neuroscience*, **11**(**9**). http://doi.org /10.3389/fnbeh.2017.00009

Nöth, W. (2001). Ecosemiotics and the semiotics of nature. *Sign Systems Studies*, **29**(**1**), 71–81.

Nöth, W. (2014). The life of symbols and other legisigns: More than mere metaphor? In V. Romanini and E. Fernández, eds., *Peirce and Biosemiotics: A Guess at the Riddle of Life*. Dordrecht: Springer, 171–82.

Nöth, W. (2018). The semiotics of models. *Sign Systems Studies*, **46**(**1**), 7–43.

Odling-Smee, J., Laland, K. N. and Feldman, M. W. (2003) *Niche Construction: The Neglected Process in Evolution*. Princeton: Princeton University Press.

Ojamaa, M. and Torop, P. (2015). Transmediality of cultural autocommunication. *International Journal of Cultural Studies*, **18**(**1**), 61–78.

Oliver, M. (1992). *New and Selected Poems. Vol 1*. Boston, MA: Beacon Press.

Palagi, E., Nicotra, V. and Cordoni, G. (2015). Rapid mimicry and emotional contagion in domestic dogs. *Royal Society Open Science*, **2**(**12**), 150505. http://doi.org/10.1098/rsos.150505.

Patoine, P.-L. and Hope, J. (2015). The semiosphere, between informational modernity and ecological postmodernity. *Recherches sémiotiques / Semiotic Inquiry (RS/SI)*, **35**(**1**), 11–26.

Patten, B. C. and Odum, E. P. (1981). The cybernetic nature of ecosystems. *The American Naturalist*, **118**(**6**), 886–95.

Peh, K. S.-H., Corlett, R. T. and Bergeron, Y., eds. (2015). *Routledge Handbook of Forest Ecology*. London: Routledge.

Peirce, C. S. (1958–1966). *Collected papers. Vols. 1–6 edited by Charles Hartshorne and Paul Weiss; vols. 7–8 edited by A. W. Burks*. Cambridge, MA: Belknap Press of Harvard University Press (referred as CP).

Perlmutter, D. (ed.) (2019). *The Microbiome and the Brain*. Boca Raton: CRC Press.

Peterson, J. V., Thornburg, A. M., Kissel, M. et al. (2018). Semiotic mechanisms underlying niche construction. *Biosemiotics*, **11**, 181–98.

Petrilli, S. (2003). Modeling, dialogue, and globality: Biosemiotics and semiotics of self. 2. Biosemiotics, semiotics of self, and semioethics. *Sign Systems Studies*, **31**(**1**), 65–105.

Petrilli, S. and Ponzio, A. (2005). *Semiotics Unbounded: Interpretive Routes through the Open Network of Signs*. Toronto: University of Toronto Press.

Piiper, J. (1935). *Pilte ja hääli kodumaa loodusest I [Images and sounds from homeland's nature I]*. Tartu: Noor-Eesti.

Piiper, J. (1968). *Rännakuid Eesti radadel [Wanderings in Estonian routes]*. Tallinn: Eesti Raamat.

Pilgrim, S. and Pretty, J. (2013). Nature and culture: An introduction. In S. Pilgrim and J. Pretty, eds., *Nature and Culture. Rebuilding Lost Connections*. Oxon: Routledge, 1–20.

Polanyi, M. (1966). *The Tacit Dimension*. Chicago: The University of Chicago Press.

Polanyi, M (1967). Sense-giving and sense-reading. *Philosophy*, **42(162)**, 301–25.

Posner, R. (2000). Semiotic pollution. *Sign Systems Studies*, **28**, 290–307.

Proops, L. and McComb, K. (2010). Attributing attention: the use of human-given cues by domestic horses (Equus caballus). *Animal Cognition*, **13**, 197–205.

Puura, I. (2013). Nature in our memory. *Sign Systems Studies*, **41(1)**, 150–3.

Raffa, K. F., Aukema, B. H., Bentz, B. J., Carroll, A. L., Hicke, J. A., Turner, M. G. and Romme, W. H. (2008). Cross-scale drivers of natural disturbances prone to anthropogenic amplification: The dynamics of bark beetle eruptions. *BioScience*, **58(6)**, 501–17.

Remm, T. (2015). *Sociocultural Space: Spatial Modelling and the Sociocultural World. Dissertationes Semioticae Universitatis Tartuensis 20*. Tartu: University of Tartu Press.

Rueckert, W. (1978). Literature and ecology: An experiment in ecocriticism. *Iowa Review*, **9(1)**, 71–86.

Sánchez-García, F. J., Machado, V., Galián, J. and Gallego, D. (2017). Application of the eco-field and general theory of resources to bark beetles: Beyond the niche construction theory. *Biosemiotics*, **10**, 57–73.

Sebeok, T. A. (1981). *The Play of Musement*. Bloomington: Indiana University Press.

Sebeok, T. A. (1990). *Essays in Zoosemiotics (Monograph Series of the TSC 5)*. Toronto: Toronto Semiotic Circle; Victoria College in the University of Toronto.

Sebeok, T. A. (1991). In what sense is language a "primary modeling system"? In *A Sign is Just a Sign*. Bloomington: Indiana University Press, 49–58.

Sebeok, T. A. (2001). Tell me, where is fancy bred? The biosemiotic self. In *Global Semiotics*. Bloomington: Indiana University Press, 120–7.

Sebeok, T. A. and Danesi, M. (2000). *The Forms of Meaning: Modeling Systems Theory and Semiotic Analysis*. Berlin: Mouton de Gruyter.

Sell, R. D. (2000). *Literature as Communication: The Foundations of Meditating Criticism*. Amsterdam: John Benjamins.

Serres, M. (2007). *The Parasite*. Minneapolis: University of Minnesota Press.

Serres, M. (2011). *Malfeasance: Appropriation Through Pollution?* Stanford: Stanford University Press.

Siewers, A. (2011). Pre-modern ecosemiotics: The green world as literary ecology. In T. Peil, ed., *The Space of Culture – The Place of Nature in Estonia and Beyond*. Tartu: University of Tartu Press, 39–68.

Siewers, A. (2014). Introduction: song, tree, and spring: environmental meaning and environmental humanities. In A. Siewers, ed., *Re-imagining nature: environmental humanities and ecosemiotics*, Bucknell: Bucknell University Press, 1–41.

Slabbekoorn, H. and Halfwerk, W. (2009). Behavioural ecology: Noise annoys at community level. *Current Biology*, **19**(**16**), R693–R695.

Sonesson, G. (2010). From mimicry to mime by way of mimesis: Reflections on a general theory of iconicity. *Sign Systems Studies*, **38**(**1**), 18–66.

Spretnak, C. (1997). *The Resurgence of the Real: Body, Nature, and Place in a Hypermodern World*. Reading, MA: Addison-Wesley.

Stachowicz, J. J. (2001). Mutualism, facilitation, and the structure of ecological communities. *Bioscience*, **51**(**3**), 235–46.

Stibbe, A. (2012). *Animals Erased: Discourse, Ecology and Reconnection with the Natural World*. Middletown: Wesleyan University Press.

Stibbe, A. (2015). *Ecolinguistics: Language, Ecology and the Stories We Live By*. London: Routledge.

Stock, A. K., Dajkic, D., Köhling, H. L., von Heinegg, E. H., Fiedler, M. and Beste, C. (2017). Humans with latent toxoplasmosis display altered reward modulation of cognitive control. *Scientific Reports*, **7**(**1**), 10170.

Suzuki, T. N. (2016). Semantic communication in birds: Evidence from field research over the past two decades. *Ecological Research* 31(3): 307–19.

Tobias, J. A., Planqué, R., Cram, D. L. and Seddon, N. (2014). Species interactions and the structure of complex communication networks. *Proceedings of the National Academy of Sciences of the United States of America*, **111**(**3**), 1020–5.

Tondl, L. (2000). Semiotic foundation of models and modelling. In J. Bernard, P. Grzybek and G. Withalm, eds., *Modellierungen von Geschichte und Kultur Modelling History and Culture Akten des 9. Internationalen Symposiums der Osterreichischen Gesellschaft fur Semiotik Universitat Graz, 22.–24. November 1996 Band I. Angewandte Semiotik 16/17*. Wien: OGS, 81–9.

Tønnessen, M. (2014). Umwelt trajectories. *Semiotica*, **198**, 159–80.

Torop, P. (2008). Translation as communication and auto-communication. *Sign Systems Studies*, **36**(**2**), 375–96.

Tüür, K. (2009). Bird sounds in nature writing: human perspective on animal communication. *Sign Systems Studies*, **37**(**3/4**), 226–55.

Tüür, K. (2016). Semiotics of textual animal representations. In T. Maran, M. Tønnessen and S. Rattasepp, eds., *Animal Umwelten in a Changing World: Zoosemiotic Perspectives (Tartu Semiotics Library; 18)*. Tartu: University of Tartu Press, 222–38.

Uexküll, J. von (1982). The theory of meaning. *Semiotica*, **42**, 25–82.

Van Dyck, H. (2012). Changing organisms in rapidly changing anthropogenic landscapes: the significance of the 'Umwelt'-concept and functional habitat for animal conservation. *Evolutionary Applications*, **5**(2), 144–53.

Veivo, H., Ljungberg, C. and Johansen, J. D. (eds.) (2009). *Redefining Literary Semiotics*. Newcastle upon Tyne: Cambridge Scholars Publishing.

Vernatsky, V. (1997). *Biosphere*. New York: Copernicus.

Vladimirova, E. (2009). Sign activity of mammals as means of ecological adaptation. *Sign Systems Studies*, **37**(3/4), 614–38.

Weik von Mossner, A. (2018). Green states of mind? Cognition, emotion and environmental framing. *Green Letters*, **22**(3), 313–23.

West-Eberhard, M. (2003). *Developmental Plasticity and Evolution*. Oxford: Oxford University Press.

Westling, L. (2016). Dangerous intersubjectivities from Dionysos to Kanzi. In M. Tønnessen, K. Armstrong Oma and S. Rattasepp, eds., *Thinking about Animals in the Age of the Anthropocene*. Lanham: Lexington Books, 19–36.

Wheeler, W. (2006). *The Whole Creature: Complexity, Biosemiotics and the Evolution of Culture*. London: Lawrence & Wishart.

Wheeler, W. (2016). *Expecting the Earth. Life, Culture, Biosemiotics*. London: Lawrence & Wishart.

Woodward F. I. (1994). How many species are required for a functional ecosystem? In E. D. Schulze and H. A. Mooney, eds., *Biodiversity and Ecosystem Function. (Praktische Zahnmedizin Odonto-Stomatologie Pratique Practical Dental Medicine (Geology), vol. 99)* Berlin: Springer, 271–92.

Zaliznjak, A. A., Ivanov, V. V. and Toporov, V. N. (1978). Structural-typological study of semiotic modeling systems. In D. P. Lucid, ed., *Soviet Semiotics: An Anthology*. Baltimore: Johns Hopkins University Press, 47–58.

Acknowledgments

This Element would have not materialized without many good partners of dialogue. I would like to express my gratitude to all my colleagues at the Department of Semiotics, University of Tartu, Estonia, and especially to those who have contributed to the development of ecosemiotics in Tartu: Kalevi Kull, Riin Magnus, Nelly Mäekivi, Silver Rattasepp, Renata Sõukand, Kati Lindström, and Kadri Tüür. I am grateful to Almo Farina, Louise Westling, Morten Tønnessen, Karel Kleisner, and Wendy Wheeler for inspiration and encouragement over the years. I also thank Ene-Reet Soovik for her advice on language issues and the anonymous reviewers for their constructive feedback. The research for this Element was supported by the Estonian Research Council (individual group research grant PRG314 "Semiotic fitting as a mechanism of biocultural diversity: Instability and sustainability in novel environments" and individual research grant PUT1363 "Semiotics of multispecies environments: Agencies, meaning making and communication conflicts").

Cambridge Elements ≡

Environmental Humanities

Louise Westling
University of Oregon

Louise Westling is an American scholar of literature and environmental humanities who was a founding member of the Association for the Study of Literature and Environment and its President in 1998. She has been active in the international movement for environmental cultural studies, teaching and writing on landscape imagery in literature, critical animal studies, biosemiotics, phenomenology, and deep history.

Serenella Iovino
University of North Carolina at Chapel Hill

Serenella Iovino is Professor of Italian Studies and Environmental Humanities at the University of North Carolina at Chapel Hill. She has written on a wide range of topics, including environmental ethics and ecocritical theory, bioregionalism and landscape studies, ecofeminism and posthumanism, comparative literature, eco-art, and the Anthropocene.

Timo Maran
University of Tartu

Timo Maran is an Estonian semiotician and poet. Maran is Professor of Ecosemiotics and Environmental Humanities and Head of the Department of Semiotics at the University of Tartu. His research interests are semiotic relations of nature and culture, Estonian nature writing, zoosemiotics and species conservation, and semiotics of biological mimicry.

About the Series

The environmental humanities is a new transdisciplinary complex of approaches to the embeddedness of human life and culture in all the dynamics that characterize the life of the planet. These approaches reexamine our species' history in light of the intensifying awareness of drastic climate change and ongoing mass extinction. To engage this reality, Cambridge Elements in Environmental Humanities builds on the idea of a more hybrid and participatory mode of research and debate, connecting critical and creative fields.

Cambridge Elements ≡

Environmental Humanities

Elements in the Series

Printed in the United States
By Bookmasters